Pharn

Landing

How To Land the Pharmaceutical Sales Job You Want —and Succeed In It!

Second Edition

FRANK A. MELFA

Power Writings

Published by: Power Writings
9019 Wall Street North Bergen, NJ 07047

Publisher's Cataloging-in-Publication
(Provided by Quality Books, Inc.)

Melfa, Frank A. Pharmaceutical Landing: How to Land the Pharmaceutical Sales Job You Want--and Succeed In It! / Frank A. Melfa.
p. cm. Includes bibliographical references and index.

LCCN 2007932345
ISBN 978-0-9641640-8-6

1. Pharmaceutical industry--Vocational guidance--United States. 2. Selling--Vocational guidance--United States. 3. Job hunting--United States. I. Title.

HD9666.5.M45 2005 615'.1'02373
QBI04-200492

Contents

Introduction

Some things have changed in the pharmaceutical industry since the first edition of *Pharmaceutical Landing*. Big Pharma has decreased and continues to decrease their sales forces. They figured out that doctors don't want to see several sales reps from the same company promoting the same products. They also figured out that the Pod system of selling means little or no accountability. When you have three sales reps calling on the same doctors selling the same product, any of the reps can claim responsibility for the sales success of the territory. Although managers know which rep or reps are really driving the sales and which are not, reps can still get away with riding the coattails of the hardworking reps. That was my experience managing Pods. It was usually one rep responsible for the sales success of the territory. So I applaud Big Pharma for moving away from Pods, pleasing their customers, and holding reps accountable for their results.

Even with the recent changes and cuts in sales forces, there are still many job opportunities in pharmaceutical sales. When you research Career Builder, MONSTER, and Hot Jobs, you will always see pharmaceutical sales job openings throughout the country. Although Big Pharma is cutting back, smaller companies continue to launch new products and expand sales forces. There is constant turnover in pharmaceutical sales just like in any industry. People either leave voluntarily or are forced to leave. Either way, there is a constant demand for smart, hardworking salespeople.

As I mentioned in the first edition of *Pharmaceutical Landing*, pharmaceutical sales representatives can easily earn $100,000 or more a year. This ranks them in the top ten percent of wage earners in the U.S. Successful sales representatives—the ones who work hard every day, become product experts and have great attitudes—can earn more than $100,000 a year. With an average starting base salary of $55,000, quarterly bonuses, stock options, cars, and career advancement, it's no wonder that thousands of people continue to compete for these jobs every day.

I left Big Pharma and worked for a small company where my reps' average bonus was $8,500 each quarter. That's $34,000 a year, doubled the average bonus of most pharma companies. My top reps made between $15,000 to $20,000, each quarter or $60,000 to $80,000 a year in bonus alone!

SUCCESS FOR THE FEW

At most companies, only 10% of the sales representatives receive the top sales awards known through the industry as President's Club. Some of those awards include trips, cash awards, car upgrade, additional stock options, salary increases, and other incentives. Other reps either produce average results or lose their jobs within a year. Some learn that they can't do the job and others just don't want to do the job. If you are interested in doing this job right, then *Pharmaceutical Landing* will help launch you to the top 10% if you are willing to learn and work for it.

Pharmaceutical companies pay well because being a pharmaceutical sales rep is hard work. After a full day of calling on at least nine to ten doctors, attending educational dinner programs, then checking e-mails and voicemails, a day could run past 11:00 p.m. When I was a district manager for a Big Pharma company, we received about five hundred résumés a week for every open sales position. We disregarded about ninety percent of those résumés and few candidates made it past the first round of interviews. At job fairs, if we interviewed one hundred people, we asked back less than 10% for second interviews and of that 10%, we may have hired one person. Why do so few people make it past the first interview? It's probably the same reason many pharmaceutical reps don't succeed—they just wing it! For starters, candidates' résumés are not pharmaceutically focused and candidates don't prepare for interviews—just like the average and below-average pharmaceutical sales reps that don't prepare for sales calls and just wing it.

COMMON MISTAKES:

- Most candidates do not prepare for interviews and rely too much on the Internet for their research. Although the Internet is a good starting point, the focus of the research should be on interviewing doctors, pharmacists, and pharmaceutical sales representatives. Candidates need to do things the job itself entails, so when a hiring manager asks them what they did to prepare for the interview, they will have something different and significant to say rather than just discuss an internet search. Even with Internet access to company information, many candidates know little about the company and its products and still expect to get asked back for a second interview.

- Many people want these jobs, but yet have no idea

of what a pharmaceutical salesperson does every day. During interviews some candidates ask me what a typical day is like for a pharmaceutical rep. I'm either thinking or saying depending on what mood they catch me in, "that's what you should be telling me." How can you want a job and not know what a typical day of that job involves?

- Some tell me that they have friends in the industry, but few show the foresight to spend a day in the field with that friend to learn and experience the job.

- Candidates need to show that they can sell. If you have prior sales experience, then show us what you sold and how you sold it. Come prepared with sales results and ranking reports.

- Regardless of sales experience, candidates who do not ask for the job or a second interview won't usually get it. This is a sales job—salespeople succeed by asking for things.

I have as little patience with people who do not prepare for interviews as with salespeople who do not perform. When you hear me say, "Do you have any questions for me?" within the first ten minutes of the interview, then you know it's over. When reps continue to produce lousy sales results, make excuses, and do nothing different in the field, then it's over for them too.

If you are looking for a book to show you the "nice" way to land a pharmaceutical sales job and succeed in it, then search for another book, because this is the no-nonsense approach! That is, learning to go the extra mile—the way that may be painful, the way that will help you get ahead of the competition.

Now it's up to you. Let me first help you land a job and then show you how to be successful. For those of you who have already landed a pharmaceutical sales job, there is always something new you can learn.

In *Pharmaceutical Landing*, I review common mistakes candidates make during the interview process, how to properly prepare for both job fairs and formal interviews, and what managers look for in candidates. I also discuss why the top 10% of pharmaceutical sales reps consistently succeed in their jobs and why most don't. Once you land your job, I'll show you how to do it right.

Throughout the book, please keep in mind that I sometimes use fictitious product names when discussing selling examples.

Chapter One

Pharmaceutical Landing

THE INTERVIEW

B E ON T IME!

The first thing I'll say about interviewing for a pharmaceutical sales job, or for any job, is to be on time. As far as I'm concerned, there is no excuse for being late. About 30 to 40% percent of candidates are either late for interviews or don't show up at all. I would never offer a job to anyone who is late for an interview. I find people's behavior during the interview process to be consistent to what they do during the job. If a candidate is late for an interview, then they will usually be late to meetings and field rides with their managers.

Once you have confirmed the interview location, do not ask your potential manager or interviewer for directions! Once again this is a sign of resourcefulness. Either call the hotel or look up the location and directions yourself.

Arrive an hour early. Sit in your car, drink coffee, review your notes, and practice what you want to say during the interview. This time cushion also allows room for possible traffic delays, a flat tire, or even getting lost, all excuses that I have heard and never accept.

During a day of interviews, I was looking for my next candidate. She was already five minutes late. I noticed a missed call on my cell phone and dialed it. A woman answered from a service station. I asked her if she had just seen a young woman dressed in a business suit. She told me that a nice young woman with red hair had used her phone to call a cab because her car had broken down up the road, and that she had left about fifteen minutes before.

Then the voice on the other end of the phone erupted into laughter. I asked her why she was laughing. She first apologized, and then told me she had noticed the redheaded young woman had a long rip in her stocking. Laughing myself, I asked her which leg, just so I could verify the claim. She told me it was the right leg and then erupted again.

About twenty minutes later, I decided to walk around the hotel to try to find the redhead with the rip in her right stocking. Sure enough, I found her walking in the back entrance of the hotel. She told me she had just paid $250 for a cab. Of course, I admired her persistence paying the money to get to the interview. She was going to get a fair shot at convincing me to hire her.

Sometimes incidents like these help demonstrate people's tenacity. On the other hand, if she had planned to arrive an hour early, she would have arrived on time for the interview, with a great story about the flat tire that would have showed her persistence, tenacity and foresight.

As I led her to my interviewing spot, I told her that I had spoken to the service station person, just to reassure her that I knew her story was true. As she walked ahead of me to sit down, I thought about the laughing woman on the phone and couldn't resist. Sure enough, there it was, a vertical rip in her right stocking. I smiled, fought back my laughter, and couldn't wait to start this interview!

To give her time to settle down and organize herself, I walked to the front desk of the hotel and brought her back a bottle of water. During the interview, I learned the car breakdown wasn't an isolated incident. Her résumé was spattered with coffee stains; she ruffled through papers crunched in a dirty folder; and she knew nothing about my company or the products. Although I was entertained and developed a genuine liking for this person, she didn't make it past this interview.

To avoid getting lost and being late, plan ahead. Drive or take public transportation to the interview location a day or two before the interview. This shows foresight and good planning skills. Many interviewers break the ice by asking about the drive to the interview locations. In this case, an icebreaker question can turn out to be an interview question that benefits you, because you get to show your potential manager that you are smart enough to plan ahead. What most of you don't realize is the interview starts as soon as you walk through the door.

Most interviews take place in hotels. After sipping coffee and reviewing your notes in your car, plan to walk through the lobby doors about 15 minutes before the interview. Try to avoid walking in any earlier or any later than that. If you want to make a good impression, showing the interviewer that you had the foresight to arrive an hour early, you can always mention it during the interview, regardless of whether the interviewer asks or not. You would already be selling yourself.

There are reasons you would not want to arrive more than 15 minutes early. During my first day of interviewing as a district manager, one of my colleagues showed me how to "candidate-watch." We were interviewing on the second floor of a hotel, overlooking the lobby. After each interview, my colleague and I would lean over the railing and watch the candidates in the lobby. We noticed some candidates reviewing notes, some reading books (we were hoping to see sales books and not Danielle Steel novels), while others frantically searched for us by walking around the lobby initiating discussions with other people. These were all good signs.

Those who were sitting down with their legs crossed, reading a newspaper, could be viewed as lacking a sense of urgency. We like the type "A" people, the ones who scurry around the lobby eager to get started. To avoid any possible misperceptions, try not to walk through the hotel doors more than fifteen minutes early. On the other hand, you don't want to walk through the doors right on-time. As far as I'm concerned arriving on-time is late. So play it safe and walk through the doors 15 minutes early.

FIND ME

Once you enter the hotel doors (hopefully 15 minutes early), start looking for your interviewer. Don't just sit down. Walk around and approach anyone who might be the interviewer. Stand in the middle of the lobby and make eye contact with people until someone reciprocates.

Sometimes I sit near the hotel entrance, working on my laptop, just to see if the interviewee will make an effort to approach me. Some candidates make no effort at all. They sit and wait to be approached. Timid people usually don't make it in sales. I need people who are not afraid to walk into a doctor's office and talk to everyone—to be the mayor!

During an interview at the New York Hilton on 6th Avenue and 53rd Street, I sat in the lounge facing the front doors of the main lobby, where I could see everyone who walked in. When I had spoken to the candidate earlier in the morning, she had described herself as tall, with blond hair, and said that she would be wearing a black suit. After I described myself as, short Italian from New Jersey, we agreed to meet in the lobby at 1:00 p.m. At 12:45, people were scampering in and out of the front doors, making it difficult for me to see. However, I would have noticed a tall blond woman if she had been walking around trying to find someone.

Many people were sitting on a circular sofa positioned in front of the lobby doors. Between 12:59 and 1:01 p.m., I noticed a blond woman wearing a black suit sitting on the circular sofa. I must have missed her arrival. Whether she had walked in at 12:59 or 1:01 wouldn't have made much of a difference. She was late regardless.

On occasion, she would move her head from side to side, as if she was looking for someone, but that was the extent of her effort. I was thinking that if that was the candidate, how could she expect me to find her sitting in a crowded lobby? I sat for a few minutes to see if she would make an effort to look for me, then finally gave up and approached her. Sure enough, it was she. As I write, I can't remember anything specific about that interview, which makes me believe she did not impress me.

During another recent interview at the same hotel, I was interviewing final candidates as the national sales director of a new pharmaceutical company I had recently joined. I told the candidates to meet me in the lobby. I sat facing the entrance and watched a young man walked towards the lobby who appeared to be my candidate. I was sitting at a small table with a folder and his resume on the table. There were about three or four other people sitting around me, but most people would figure I was the interviewer since I was wearing a suit, sitting by myself, and had a manila folder and paper on the table. I had "interviewer" written all over me. So I thought. As he approached the area where I was sitting, I stared right at him with my chin up as if to say, "Hey, it's me." He didn't even look my way. He didn't appear to be looking for anyone. His lack of communication made me think maybe it wasn't him after all. He then sat down at a table and pulled out the New York Times. I then thought there was no way this was my candidate and if it was, he had just bombed his interview before even meeting me. He then stood up and walked away again making no attempt to communicate with anyone. About five minutes later and also five minutes until the official start of the interview, he walked back towards me and again I made eye contact and looked his way. He finally looked at me and asked if I was Frank. Finally, I thought. I didn't think it was worth asking why he didn't ask me before. If I have to ask questions like that, then I'm sure that the candidate is not the right person for the job.

I interviewed him for about twenty minutes before I asked him if he had any questions for me. His question floored me more than his lack of communication I described earlier. He asked me what my position was with my company!

I asked another candidate to meet me at the LaGuardia Marriott in New York at 7:00 a.m. I arrived at 6:00 a.m. to beat the traffic and to "candidate-watch." I sat near the front entrance of the lobby, working on my laptop and drinking coffee while I waited. At about 6:55, I walked around the lobby looking at my watch and making eye contact with everyone, until a young man finally met my eyes. After we introduced ourselves, he told me he had arrived about forty minutes before and had seen me getting coffee. I asked him why he hadn't approached me. He had no answer. He also did not interview well.

You cannot be afraid to approach people. If you want to be in pharmaceutical sales, you are going to need to crawl out of your shell. Always be talking and selling. You can practice now by greeting and talking to people when you normally wouldn't. Say hello to people no matter where you are.

When I sold in hospitals, I would sell in the elevator, the cafeteria—whether doctors were on line buying lunch or sitting down eating. I would sell in the library or in the parking lot. I would talk with the valet people who parked my car. Be a good person and be nice to everyone and be genuine about it.

BE NICE TO EVERYONE

One of my former managers would tell candidates to check in at the front desk of the hotel before an interview. He would provide the front-desk people with a spreadsheet that included the candidates' names. They would rate each candidate's friendliness on a scale of one through five. This proved to be a valuable part of the interview process. A candidate who was rude to hotel personnel already had one strike against him. We want to hire people who are genuinely friendly to everyone. So be nice to everyone and not just to the people you think are important.

BE PREPARED

Don't rely on your good looks and personality to land a job. Don't laugh—I had at least two people tell me that I should have hired them because doctors liked seeing pretty reps. One candidate even pointed to her face while saying it. There's much more to it than that—for instance, being prepared. I can't believe how many people show up to interviews unprepared. There are a few that don't even wear a business suit, but the ones that dumbfound me are those referred to me by my own salespeople. These people have great advantages over other candidates. As well as a guaranteed interview, they have access to product literature, insights about the job, and information about me. I would tell my salespeople not to coach them unless they specifically asked for help. I want to know if candidates have the foresight to act on this major advantage on their own by asking the sales reps for product literature and information.

WHAT ABOUT THE PRODUCTS?

"I really want to work for your company." Many tell me this, yet most of them can't tell me a thing about the products they would be selling. Sure, they might be able to tell me about the history of the company, but I don't care about the history—tell me about the products! Show me sales literature, a sample box, an ad, and then sell me. Most people have no clue of what the job entails, yet they claim to be certain that it's what they want to do.

I was interviewing a young man who initially struck me as being confident and aggressive. This was his first interview with me, but his second interview with my company, so I expected him to be fully prepared to discuss our products.

He told me that his mother was a gynecologist, so I asked him what he knew about our flagship gynecological product, which then was the number-one written branded drug in the United States. I was amazed that he couldn't tell me anything about the product. All he had to do was ask his mother. I'm sure she had prescribed it every day that week. He hadn't had the foresight to talk with his mother about a company he might be working for and hadn't even thought to ask during his first interview about what products he would be selling. He was no more prepared for this interview than he had been for the first.

My next question was, "Do you have any questions for me?" (I usually ask that question to end the interview.) If I ask that question within the first ten to fifteen minutes, it is not a good sign. When I interview final candidates for my district managers, they notice me putting my pen back in my pocket, understanding that I am through with the interview. If that happens within the first ten to fifteen minutes, it is also not a good sign.

The more you know about the products, the better. But it also depends on the situation. If you are attending a job fair with many pharmaceutical companies, then you could get away with a brief summary of a company's top-selling products. During job fairs, the interviews will often be short. When you land that second interview, then you'd better be fully prepared. Forget the history lesson (when and how the Company got started) and be ready to discuss the Company's products and the competing products as well.

Here is an example of what to discuss about a pharmaceutical product during an interview:

- Drug A is an ACE inhibitor that was originally FDA-approved to treat hypertension, but is now the only ACE that is proven and indicated to prevent the risk of cardiovascular events.

- ACE inhibitors work by preventing angiotensin I from converting to angiotensin II which increases vasodilatation which helps decrease blood pressure.

- Drug A is the only ACE inhibitor with a landmark trial that showed that adding it to other agents further reduced the risk of cardiovascular events.

The trial was published in the *New England Journal Medicine* in January of 2002. It evaluated over 9000 high-risk patients. (If you come prepared with the actual trial, as opposed to a summary of it from the Internet, and use a few bullets, you would impress the hell out of me.)

GET OFF THE INTERNET AND DO SOMETHING THAT THE JOB ENTAILS!

Visit a Doctor

The Internet is a good starting point to research a company and its products, but it shouldn't end there. The meat of your research should focus on talking with doctors and pharmacists. This is what the job entails. So when a district manager asks you what you did to prepare for the interview, you will have plenty to say.

If you want to guarantee yourself a second interview or even the job, visit doctors in their offices. Ask the receptionist if you could speak with the doctor. Be prepared with questions. The doctors will provide you with information about how they use the products to treat their patients. The receptionist could provide you with sample boxes of the drugs you would be selling— great props to use during the interview.

Contact a Salesperson

Office managers can also provide you with business cards of pharmaceutical reps. A pharmaceutical rep could land you an interview with his district manager as well as insights into the job and the company's products.

If you already have an interview set up with a company, the receptionist could provide you with business cards of that company's pharmaceutical reps. Those salespeople can provide you with information about the company, its products, and the hiring manager. If you impress a salesperson, you could also earn a recommendation from that person. Managers value the opinions of their salespeople. Most of our hires come from internal referrals. A salesperson can earn a fee of about $2000 for every person they refer who gets hired.

Visit Your Local Pharmacist

Visit a local pharmacy and discuss products with a pharmacist. Once again, the pharmacist could provide valuable information about the products and company. More importantly, a pharmacist could provide you with the prescribing habits of local doctors. You can then visit doctors who use the drugs that you would be selling. Those doctors would have more positive things to say about the products you would be selling.

SHOW & SELL!

During my first pharmaceutical job interview, I brought in a first aid kit for golfers that I had developed and sold in my previous job. I also brought in an autographed copy of my self-published book, *Bodybuilding: A Realistic Approach*, to my soon-to-be manager. I showed him why my book was the best-selling bodybuilding book on Amazon.com. I whipped out my pen and pointed to the photographs on the cover, explaining the realistic approach to bodybuilding. He was also an avid golfer (at least he thought he was). If I had to do it again, I would have sold him the golfer's kit rather than just show it to him. I could have said, "Do you see the advantage of having this kit in your golf bag? Have you ever gotten sunburned? Did you ever cut your hand on the course and wish you had a band-aid? OK, then, do you have five dollars to pay for it now? Will you buy it?"

I'm not saying you have to write and sell your own book, or create a product, but at least bring something to the interview to sell besides yourself and your résumé. I notice many people bring a leather carrying case to interviews. I usually ask people what they have inside, just in case they had prepared something and feel timid about showing it to me. Some people have notes and other information they had gathered, while most have nothing except the fancy leather carrying case.

Most people who prepare notes and get other information think they need to memorize it. Managers don't expect salespeople to memorize literature when discussing it with a doctor. Why should we expect it of you? We expect our salespeople to show doctors literature and other selling aids during a sales call (*See Fundamental 3, Effective Use of Literature in Chapter Three).*

I'm impressed when candidates whip out their notes and other props, move close to me, and start selling, using a pen to point. This shows that you have done your homework and that you can sell. If we don't ask you to show us anything during the interview, be aggressive and show us anyway. A doctor isn't going to ask you to show them anything.

Brag Books

If you have been successful in your current or previous job, particularly sales, then bring your brag book. If you don't have a brag book, then make one, unless of course you have nothing to brag about. Not only will you get the opportunity to show off your sales numbers, but you also get to show good organizational skills and an opportunity to sell yourself and your accomplishments

Good candidates bring an organized binder with sales reports, letters of recommendation, award letters, and other documents. They take me through it page-by-page. Seasoned sales people pull a pen out of their pocket and start pointing to their accomplishments while maintaining eye contact.

Understand the Sales Reports!

If you are showing sales reports that highlight your accomplishments, be sure to understand the reports. I'm amazed that candidates don't know how to read a simple sales report. I start asking questions about the reports and people start sweating. Some candidates don't know the time period the reports cover, market share, or the criteria for rankings. I'm most amazed with candidates with pharmaceutical sales experience that don't know the difference between new prescriptions and total prescriptions. Practice presenting each page of your brag book as you would present a product to a client or doctor.

I always ask candidates with prior sales experience to show me a brag book, especially to back up sales performance and awards listed on their résumés. I want to see proof from the brag book or the actual awards. Some candidates tell me that they left their brag book or sales reports at home and that they will bring them next time. Little do they know there won't be a next-time!

JOB FAIRS

Outside companies usually organize job fairs that take place in hotels. This differs from an "open house" which is usually set up and presented by a single pharmaceutical company. You will find many companies at job fairs. The set-up company screens candidates based on the minimal requirements of each company.

Most pharmaceutical companies require a bachelor's degree, at least one year of sales experience, or a science background. The minimal requirements of the pharmaceutical company will determine which booth the set-up company will allow you to visit. They will stamp the back of your résumé with the company's name. If we do not see that stamp, then theoretically, we should not interview you.

Here is where you start selling. You can try to persuade

the set-up company person to stamp your resume, even though you may not fulfill all the minimum requirements. You can also visit the pharmaceutical sales booths and sell a manager to interview you, even though the set-up company didn't stamp your resume. I have never refused to interview someone at a job fair. Most district managers appreciate the selling effort.

After the stamp of approval by the set-up company, you would sign in at the pharmaceutical company's booth and wait for someone to call your name. Once you are face-to-face with a district manager, you'd better start selling. You will only have about five to ten minutes to sell yourself. We will ask some basic questions such as, "Why pharmaceutical sales?" Or "Why should I consider you?" The rest you should initiate. Be prepared to discuss your accomplishments and your desire to work in pharmaceutical sales. In this short period of time, we evaluate your ability to sell. The more you sell us, the more time you earn. We may ask you about a specific selling situation. Lacking sales experience will put you at a disadvantage, but if you come prepared and show us that you have the ability to sell, then you will get a fair shot.

As I mentioned before, we won't expect you to have elaborate knowledge about our products at a job fair. You could however learn which companies will be at the job fair and do some research on each of the companies and their best-selling products. You could even do a short Internet search at the hotel before visiting the booths. Knowing something about each company and their products at a job fair will gain you a big advantage over the other candidates.

Your main objective at a job fair is to get a second interview. This could be with either the hiring manager or with another district manager at the job fair. At any interview, you should always ask yourself, "what's the goal of this interview?" A goal at a job fair will be different from a goal at a formal or second interview. The goal of the job fair is to get the second interview. The goal of a formal interview will be either ask and get the job or ask and get the final interview with the sales director. At a job fair, candidates often ask me in an attempt to close me, what the next step is. I usually tell them one of two things:

If I'm interested in a candidate, I will tell them the next step is to meet with me again or with another manager. Most candidates leave it at that. If they don't ask for the second interview, I don't ask them back.

If I'm not interested in the candidate, I tell that person the managers will decide whom we will ask back. If you hear that, then you probably won't be asked back.

When I was a district manager and I was considering asking someone back for a second interview I would run that candidate by another district manager at the job fair for a second opinion. If I liked someone but they didn't live near my opening in my district, then I would send that person to the manager with an opening in his district. Always ask if there are open territories, where they are, and if the hiring managers are at the job fair.

We look for people with dynamic personalities. After screening about twenty candidates at a job fair in New York City, I took a bathroom break. As I was walking to the bathroom, I overheard a candidate saying how bored the managers at our booth looked. At first, I was a little embarrassed, but it helped me realize that I come to life when a candidate comes to life—they smile, laugh, and tell me exciting stories about themselves. They make me remember them enough where I want to call them back.

Sometimes it is not so much what you say, but how you say it that matters. Before your interviews, practice what you want to say and how you want to say it. If you bore yourself, you can imagine how the other person across the table will feel. If you bore us, then we could safely assume you will bore a doctor and his staff.

Once we tell you, "You only have one more minute," recap your strengths and personal qualities and then close us!

TAKE NOTES

I rarely see people write anything down during interviews. I'm amazed that when I offer valuable information about the products, most people don't write down a word of it. I might say something like, "Bioflex is a statin that was originally FDA-approved to reduce cholesterol and is now indicated to reduce CV events."

I don't know many people who would know what a "statin" is unless they were taking it themselves, sold pharmaceuticals, or did the research. They look at me as if they really know what I'm talking about. I don't expect them to know, but at least to take notes and ask questions. If you show interest in the products and the foresight to ask questions and take notes, then I could see you may have a real interest in the job.

During a recent interview with a candidate, I was asking him to send me a few items to help me make a decision on whether I was going to hire him or not. When I noticed he was not writing any of my requests down, I knew right there he was not going to follow up or get hired. I even offered him my business card with my fax and e-mail information. Sure enough he did not follow up. Once again, what candidates do or don't do during the interview is usually consistent to what they will do or won't do during the job. In this case, I could have safely assumed he would not have followed up on assignments or with his doctors if I had hired him. As a district manager, I learned this lesson the hard way by letting red flags like this slide and making bad hires.

Some people ask me what I look for in a candidate. I like this question. I usually answer that I look for people with a good work ethic, proven sales ability, and for someone who is aggressive and persistent. A good candidate takes notes, summarizes these qualities back to me and provides me with specific examples of how they have demonstrated these qualities. This shows me the candidate is smart and has good listening skills. Good candidates also write me thank you notes or letters using some of the words I used during the interview.

THE MEAT OF THE INTERVIEW: THE QUESTIONS

After getting candidates to relax by asking them about the drive or something as simple as the weather, I briefly tell them about the open position and myself. I sometimes ask them to take me through their resume, just to get them comfortable talking.

When I get to the meat of the interview, I ask questions based on the candidate's resume. I evaluate only what a person has done, not what I think they *would* do. I always remind myself to stay out of the "woulds." That means avoiding questions such as, "How *would* you handle a difficult office manager?" "How many calls *would* you make every day?" People could tell me just about anything. Instead, I ask questions like, "Tell me about a time when you dealt with a difficult office manager." "What time do you start and end your day?"

You may be thinking that people could lie and tell me they start their day at 7:00 a.m. and end at 6:00 p.m., but you would be surprised. Many people consider working 10:00 a.m. to 4:00 p.m. a full workday.

Provide a STAR

The real meat of my interview involves evaluating work ethic, sales ability, persistence, tenacity, planning and organizational skills, and integrity, by using the STAR method. This means asking questions and probing into specific Situations or Tasks, in which the candidate describes specific Actions they took to complete the tasks, and the Results of those actions.

For example, when evaluating sales ability, I ask, "Can you tell me about your most memorable sales experience?" Or, "Can you give me a specific example of a big sale you made?"

The Situation

The more details you can provide about the situation, the better. I'm looking for the company name and the goal or objective of the situation. For example, you were selling a copier to XYZ Company's main office, hoping to sell copiers to all their offices in New York.

The Action

Here you need to be very specific. Tell the interviewer exactly what you did including picking up the phone, walking into the building, meeting with the gatekeeper, selling to your potential client, and closing the deal.

Did you have to get past a gatekeeper? If so, what did you do to persuade that person to let you see the decision maker? Did you bring the secretary a cup of coffee? What did you say and show the client? (*See the Mackay 66 in Chapter Four.*)

If you delivered a presentation, how did you do it? Did you use a PowerPoint presentation? Was it face-to-face? How was the room set up? How close were you to the customer? What exactly did you present? If you have a sales presentation, then sell it to the interviewer. Paint a picture of the situation. I ask my candidates to recreate the scene so I can see it. "Take me there," I would say.

The Result

"After delivering the presentation, I asked the decision-maker to buy a copier. After discussing price and shipping options, he agreed to order a copier. After that sale, I provided him with excellent customer service—constantly following up. As a result, he ordered twenty more copiers for his New York offices. That sale totaled over $100,000."

Strong candidates with solid work experience can usually provide complete STARs. Many cannot because they have no successes or relevant work experience to share. No matter how much I probe, some people can't tell me a thing. I often get general answers such as, "I would always do this," or "I would always say that."

Then I would say, "That's great, but what exactly did you do?"

"Oh, but I did it all the time."

Then I end the interview: "Do you have any questions for me?"

Here is a STAR example that includes the situation, actions, and result:

I called XYZ Company on the phone. I asked the secretary when the best day and time would be to see the owner. At first, she told me there was no best time. I then asked her how she drank her coffee and about her favorite doughnut. She told me light and sweet and chocolate coconut, so I showed up the following morning at 8:00 a.m. with her favorite doughnut and coffee. I also showed up with a car-racing magazine for the owner because Mary, the secretary, had told me the owner raced cars on weekends.

When I met Joe, the owner, we talked about cars for about twenty minutes, and then I delivered my presentation from my computer. I showed him our best copiers and what would fit best in his main office. After reviewing the features and benefits of the best copier, I asked him to buy it. He committed and we filled out the purchase order right on the spot. One week later, I followed up to make sure the copier had been delivered and was working. I asked him to buy ten more copiers for his other ten offices in New York. I closed the deal and generated $150,000 worth of business in one week.

If a candidate has no selling experience, I would say, "Tell me about a time when you had to sell an idea to your manager." This allows you to demonstrate sales ability, as long as you provide a complete STAR.

Why Pharmaceutical Sales?

This is a question I often ask and one that you will probably be asked. We want to know if this is what you really want to do. If you tell us that you have also been interviewing for a programming job or anything else unrelated to pharmaceutical sales, then you probably won't get very far in the interview process.

Here are the most common *lame* answers:

"I hear it has flexible hours."

"The industry is stable."

"It's something I have always wanted to do."

"I have friends in the industry and they tell me it's great."

"I've done some research on the industry."

If you give either of the first two answers, especially the first, you are certain not to get the job. If you want flexible hours, then work in a hair salon; they're closed on Mondays and open at 10:00 a.m.

Telling me the industry is stable doesn't tell me that you want to work in pharmaceutical sales.

If you say pharmaceutical sales is something you have always wanted to do, then show me. If you have done research, it had better be more than an Internet search. As I discussed earlier, interview pharmaceutical reps, doctors, and pharmacists. Be resourceful. Take some initiative!

If you have a friend in pharmaceutical sales, then spend a day in the field with them and be prepared to discuss what you learned. For example, tell us you learned the importance of planning a call in the car before making the call (*see Fundamental 2 in Chapter Three*). Tell us you understand the importance of the gatekeeper and learning the names of everyone in the office. Tell us about the interaction between the doctor and the salesperson. Did your friend ask the doctor questions and ask for the business?

When people tell me that they spent a day in the field with a friend, some don't remember the drugs the rep promoted. If you spend a day in the field, then take notes, get sales literature from your friend and be prepared to show the interviewer what you learned during the day.

Why Should I Hire You?

When I asked one candidate this question, she lifted her chin, pointed to her face, and said, "Because I'm very pretty and doctors like talking with pretty girls." Although appearance plays an initial role in selling, and indeed she was attractive, that wasn't exactly the answer I was looking for. Here is your last chance to sell yourself. You should practice your self-promotion before the interview. I'm amazed at how little people have to say about themselves.

Here are some personal qualities that interest me:

- Work Ethic

- Positive Attitude

- Ability to Learn Quickly

- Planning and Organizational Skills

- Persistence

- Persuasiveness

- Recognition

- Creativity

- Competitiveness

- Integrity

Here are my thoughts on some of these qualities:

Work Ethic: I want to hear that you are a hard worker. Most people don't mention having a good work ethic. I find that people who tell me they are hard workers, usually are. Of course, I would ask for specific examples of hard work. A strong work ethic is not something that is taught and it means different things to different people. Either you have it or you don't. It's something your parents instilled in you as a child. If your parents are hard workers, then there is a good chance that you are too.

I often ask candidates what time they start and end their day. Some candidates consider 10:00 a.m. to 4:00 p.m. to be a full working day. Even when candidates tell me they start at 8:00 a.m. and end at 6:00 p.m., I would prefer to hear something like this:

"I start at 7:00 a.m. and plan my day. I make my first call by 8:30 a.m. and end the day when I finish making all my planned calls. If that takes me until 6:00 p.m. or 7:00 p.m. at night, then that's when the day is over. If I finish making all my calls at 4:00 p.m., then I make extra calls that I have planned on my schedule. I don't go home until I've put in an honest day of work."

Positive Attitude: This job can be difficult at times. That's when it is most important to maintain a positive attitude. I like to hear that you are not a complainer and have the ability to bounce back after a tough call or day. You want to be the person that makes other people smile.

Ability to Learn Quickly: You also need to demonstrate that you are a quick learner and well organized. That means learning pharmacology and the products in a very short period of time. Training just teaches you the basics. You will need to plan thirty minutes each day to study your products. This takes us to planning and organization.

Planning & Organizational Skills: You may demonstrate sales ability and a good work ethic, but if you cannot plan and organize, then you will be lost in this job. You should always bring your planner or Palm Pilot to the interview. Show the interviewer that you use a planning tool. If a candidate shows up to an interview without a planner or Palm Pilot, I may not consider them. I don't care if they can sell a peace treaty to the Middle East. If they can't find the Middle East and arrive on the day of the peace meeting, then they cannot be there to sell the treaty. Many people cannot do the job because of poor organizational skills.

This job requires planning doctor calls, lunches, educational dinners, appointments, sales meetings, and many other things. Some reps forget appointments, double-book lunches and dinner programs, and miss meetings. There are also administrative tasks to organize, such as expense reports, sales reports, e-mails, product presentations, drug samples, and others.

"Tell me about a time when you had to plan an event."

If asked a question about planning, pull out your planner and show examples of something you recently planned. It could be a wedding, a party, a business meeting—anything that required using your planner and a To-Do list. Show how you prioritized your tasks by labeling them in order of importance. Show an example of how you planned your day. If you sold in a previous job, show how you scheduled customers (see Targeting and Planning in Chapter Three).

For example:

"I saw Customer A on Mondays because he was our biggest client. If I got him to order on Monday, that would give him the entire week to sell our product. With his volume of customers, he would be ready to order again on the following Monday. I saw Customer B on Tuesdays after 1:00 p.m. because he didn't see sales reps on Mondays and he always enjoyed talking to me after lunch."

Persistence: The gatekeeper may keep you from seeing the doctor, or the doctor may tell you that he won't prescribe your drug. Only persistence will get you back in that office, either to convince the gatekeeper to let you see that doctor or to sell the doctor on writing for your products. It may take five to ten visits before a doctor starts writing prescriptions for your products. You need to demonstrate a specific example when you persisted at something and succeeded.

Creativity: If you tell me that you are creative, provide me with examples. This job requires an imagination. You need to think of different ways to get by the gatekeeper. And once you get in front of the doctor, a little creativity in your presentations can help (*See Chapter Two: What it Takes!*).

Competitiveness: I remember when I first started in pharmaceutical sales, I loved getting the monthly ranking reports that ranked me out of 120 of the sales reps in the North East part of the country. I loved watching my rankings improve month over month and telling myself that I was a better salesperson than the people ranked above me. If you played sports in high school and college, be sure to mention that. Being competitive is something most managers look for during interviews.

Recognition: If you love being recognized for doing exceptional work, then don't be afraid to mention that. Salespeople live for recognition. That's why most sales organizations have incentive programs, sales contests, as well as a bonus program.

Integrity: In pharmaceutical sales, your integrity will be put to the test. You will have a corporate credit card, lunch and educational budgets, and a list of rules and regulations from the FDA, the DEA, and your company. Some people may be tempted to take advantage of the corporate credit card by using it for personal purchases. Reps have been terminated for misusing their credit cards one-way or another. Breaking sampling and DEA rules is the easiest way to lose your job. If we doubt your integrity, we will not hire you. The days of "bending the rules" are over. Provide an example of when you had to show integrity.

(See Appendix I for more interview questions and how to answer them.)

ASK FOR THE JOB!

After making it through my second, third, and fourth interviews, I was finally ready to meet the regional sales director. The final interview with the regional sales director went well until the end. I didn't ask him for the job! If you are serious about working in pharmaceutical sales, then you better learn how to close! When I spoke to my soon-to-be manager later that night, the first thing he asked me was, "Did you close him?" I hesitated and then he barked, "You didn't let him off the hook, did you? Did you ask him for the job?"

Finally I stuttered a pathetic "Nnnnoooo."

It would have been very simple. All I had to do was say something like, "Based on our discussion, will you offer me the job?" Or, "Can I have the job?" Or, "Will you hire me?" No doubt he would have said yes. Instead, I left that interview without a job. I didn't close, but it wasn't over yet.

I had read about (and discuss below) writing and hand-delivering thank you notes. Unannounced, I visited the regional director the next day at 7:00 a.m. I knew that if he was in the office that morning, then he would be the type to be in early. So at 4:45 a.m. the next morning, I drove the two-plus hours to his office.

I got lucky. At 7:00 a.m., I walked right into his office. He was raising the phone to his ear when he noticed me. At first, he looked as if he didn't know what to do with the phone. He stared at me as if he knew me from somewhere, but couldn't exactly place the face. As I started speaking, he finally surrendered the phone and the look of surprise. He was in control again.

"I just wanted to personally hand you my thank-you letter," I said as I handed it to him. "If I leave now, I should get to work in about four hours."

He was smiling, but didn't say a word. He started to open the letter, and then I just left, smiling myself. At first I was thinking: *Who's better than me?* But looking back at that experience, as great as I thought I was for hand-delivering the letter at 7:00 a.m., when it came down to it, I still didn't close him. I didn't ask him for the job! I had yet another opportunity and again, I had blown it. I just didn't get it. I had heart, but I still did not understand what it took to make it in this business. I still consider myself lucky to have gotten that job. Later, I found out that it was the letter that helped me land the job.

You will increase your chances of landing a pharmaceutical sales job when you ask for it. Most of the time, people say, "So what's the next step?" That's not a close! Even if you know the interviewer can't make a decision after the first interview, ask for the job anyway. Show your potential manager that you could close. If the next step is a second interview, then ask for it: "When can I meet with you again?" "Can we meet again tomorrow?"

Regardless of which stage of the interview process you are in, use any of the following closes:

- "Will you offer me a job?"

- "Can I have the job?"

- "Based on our interview, will you offer me the position?"

One of my favorite closes is, "Based on our interview, is

there any reason why you wouldn't offer me the job?" This allows you to overcome any objections or concerns the hiring manager may have about you.

Sales reps may ask doctors, "Is there any reason why you wouldn't use Drug X?" Sometimes, doctors provide objections, such as side effects, cost, and managed-care plans. Regardless of the objection, you need to be able to overcome it and then close again. If you don't ask a "why" question, you may not have the opportunity to overcome any concerns the hiring manager may have about you.

Once you overcome any possible concerns, be sure to ask for the job again:

- "Do you still have any concerns about me?"
- "Will you offer me the job now?"

Follow Up!

My first district manager interviewed me three times himself before sending me to another district manager and then, finally, to the regional sales director for the final interview. My manager always had something for me to do. For example, during my first interview, he suggested that I talk with some doctors and at least one pharmacist (something I should have done myself). He also told me to read *Swim With the Sharks Without Being Eaten Alive,* by Harvey Mackay and *What They Don't Teach You at Harvard Business School,* by Michael McCormack—homework I still assign to candidates. The ones who follow up with the assignments continue through the interview process.

For my follow up interview, I had called a doctor who had conducted my physical exam for my first job out of college. I still remember the Harvard Medical School certificate mounted on his wall and had wondered how much he was making as a corporate doctor after leaving private practice. I didn't think he would remember me, but I remembered that he was a funny guy. Once I got him on the phone and told him that he had conducted my physical years before, he remembered me immediately.

I told him I was interviewing for a pharmaceutical sales position and needed his help. He told me the company I was interviewing with was a leader in women's health care. He provided me with other information about products, how to dress, and how to have a sense of humor. The information itself wasn't most important, but rather the follow-up.

I interviewed another doctor and a pharmacist, and read the books by Mackay and McCormack. I wrote a brief summary of my interviews and readings and presented them during the next interview. I had passed the next round of the interview process.

During a day of interviewing, a colleague district manager and I decided to interview candidates together. We interviewed several people that day, not finding any real talent. I said to him, "When is someone going to show us something? I mean show us something they sell in their current or past sales jobs and start selling us?"

One candidate later that day answered our wish. He was referred to us by one of our own salespeople. He showed us printed marketing materials that he had created and sold to libraries and bookstores. He was selling, going through the sales presentation as if we were his customers. I complimented him, thanked him for his efforts and set him up for a second interview with another district manager. As my first district manager had done with me, I told him to get a copy of Harvey Mackay's book and be able to discuss the Mackay 66 (*See Chapter Four*). I also told him to be prepared to present two products, and to get a study. You might initially think this is too much to ask of someone on the first follow-up interview, but since this person had been referred to me by a salesperson from our company, we expected more—everything was a phone call away.

I alerted the other district manager to the assignments by faxing him a list of the tasks I had assigned the candidate. When I spoke to the district manager after the interview, I almost didn't believe him when he told me the candidate had not followed up on most of the assignments.

"You mean he didn't get the book?" I asked. "You mean he didn't get the study?"

When the candidate kept calling to ask why he hadn't heard back from me, I finally broke down and made a big mistake. I told him why he was not going to work for me. It was a mistake because he kept me on the phone for twenty minutes making excuses.

Candidates who don't follow up make excuses like, "I couldn't find the book in the bookstore," or "I ordered it online and it hasn't arrived yet." The persistent ones tell me that they tried four bookstores until they found it. One person got it from a library. People don't realize that I'm asking them to get the book as a test of their persistence as well as for their knowledge. I'm looking for persistent people who will go back to a doctor's office many times before ever seeing the doctor—those who get doors slammed in their faces and keep going back. As I mentioned before, what people do during the interview process is consistent with what they will do in the job. If they don't follow up and make excuses during the interview, then they won't follow up and make excuses during the job.

When I was typing this part of my book, I heard my old fax machine slamming and banging, shaking my desk—noises that usually waked me at night. I was thinking: *What are the chances that a candidate I interviewed at a job fair was sending me her follow-up assignment.*

My oversized fax machine started to produce her assignments, two days early. *Atta girl!* I thought. She had just made it to the next step.

I had interviewed thirty people at that job fair and asked one person to meet me the following morning at 7:30 a.m. in Brooklyn. She came prepared with her first two assignments. She showed and explained a study and discussed the two products she would be selling. She had just passed and was ready for the next step. Her next assignment was to get and read Harvey Mackay's book, type a summary about the Mackay 66, and to condense her resume from two pages to one. I told her that both assignments needed to be on my fax machine by the following Tuesday—no later.

This job requires constant follow-up. After I spent a day in the field with one of my reps, I assigned homework with specific completion dates. I never accepted excuses for incomplete tasks that were important for driving business, such as setting up educational programs, confirming a doctor's attendance at a program, inviting doctors to programs, making reservations at a restaurant, ordering a screen and projector for a presentation, following up on a doctor's request for product literature and samples, and completing expense reports on time. Those who followed-up and produced outstanding results were recognized and well rewarded. Those who did not follow up and produced lousy results did not work for me very long.

TYPE OR WRITE A THANK-YOU LETTER

"Finally, an interview seemed to go well on both sides of the desk. That had happened before and she knew she was a long way from having the job sewn up. She went back to her apartment, composed and typed a creative letter of appreciation, and hand-delivered it that same day to the maybe-boss-to-be.

*End of story? She got the job—against tough competition—
and later learned it was the letter that did the trick." (Harvey
Mackay: Lesson number 10: Short Notes Yield Long Results.)*
Business is all personal, regardless of what Michael
Corleone said in the movie the *Godfather*. Go the extra mile
and send a personalized thank-you letter. Managers and other
interviewers see many people. It's up to you to differentiate
yourself from the rest of the pack. Sending a handwritten
thank you note is a great way of doing that. Although it is a
good idea to send an immediate follow-up E-mail, follow that
up with a written note. E-mails are easy and don't impress
me. I'm not looking for a person who takes the easy road.
Handwriting or typing a thank you letter requires much more
effort than an e-mail such as using quality paper or a thank
you card, finding the interviewer's address and addressing the
envelope, searching for a stamp, and then finally mailing it.

If you really want to differentiate yourself send your thank-
you letter by Fed-Ex. This could prove to be a small investment
with a huge pay-off. Pharmaceutical sales is all about going
the extra mile. If you really want the job, then show it by taking
action!

THE SELECTION PROCESS

I interviewed candidates at least twice myself and
another manger before I sent them to my regional manager
for the final interview. That's a minimum of four interviews.
We hire candidates that have demonstrated sales ability,
persuasiveness, work ethic, ability to learn, and integrity.

Why such a cumbersome process? Because hiring is the
most important thing we do as leaders. When we hire the
wrong people (which many managers, including myself, have
done), it costs the company hundreds of thousands of dollars
in training costs and lost sales, not to mention potential

lawsuits. The key for managers is to make as few bad hires as possible. As Jim Collins mentions in his book, _Good to Great_, "Get the right people on the bus."

Sometimes it's Just My Gut

I interviewed someone four times before I decided not to hire him. He really wanted the job and was always prepared for the interviews. He knew all about the products, showed up an hour early for the first interview, followed up on every assignment, and delivered two excellent sales presentations using product literature, which he got from a doctor's office. I thought he was a perfect fit for my open territory, but even so, I wanted him to make a mistake. Something just wasn't right. I thought back through all the interviews, searching for that missing something. Then I figured it out: he didn't smile much. I could have understood if he was a little nervous, but doctors like people with great personalities. I kept picturing him in front of a doctor and just didn't see it.

Résumés

Your résumé will determine whether a manager or human resource person will call you, not hire you. It should be a brief snapshot of your career, accomplishments, and hobbies. You do not need to include your life story on it. The longer your résumé, the better chance that someone won't read it. So keep it to one page. You get to expand on your experiences and successes in person or on the phone. If I receive 100 résumés, I do not want to shuffle and read through hundreds of pages. (I will however read a cover letter.) When I read a résumé, I look for the following:

Professional: First, your résumé needs to look professional. You can use a WORD template, invest in resume software, or pay someone to do it for you. I will not call a candidate if their résumé looks like it was created on a typewriter.

- Use bullets that start with action verbs to describe what you did or do. For example,
  - *Increased copier sales*
  - *Generated revenue*
  - *Hired interns*
- Spell-check it. Have someone proof read it for you. You want to avoid typos in your résumé.

- Make sure it is easy to read: line up the dates, be consistent with fonts for each part of the résumé. For example, if your job description is italicized in one job, then all your job descriptions should be italicized.

- Make yourself accessible. Include your cell phone number as well as your work and home number. Be sure to include your e-mail address. I have thrown out many résumés because of incorrect phone numbers.

- Include complete dates: The complete dates you started and ended a job tell the interviewer to the exact time you worked a position. When we see: "*2000-2001*," for all we know, you could have worked one month. Include the month and the year! Do not skimp. If you skimp on your résumé, it could be assumed that you will skimp on the job.

Objective: If you are interviewing for a pharmaceutical

sales job then be sure to make it part of your objective. We want to hire people that want to do this job—not those exploring other opportunities. Your objective can be as simple as: *"To work in pharmaceutical sales."*

<u>Experience</u>: I read paragraphs of information and still can't figure out what candidates have done or do in their jobs. If you sold something, include what you sold and to whom you sold it. In one sentence communicate your job description. If you worked for a company for two or more years, then write a short paragraph followed by bulleted actions.

<u>Education</u>: The only time you should include your GPA is if your overall is higher than a 3.0. Otherwise don't include your GPA.

- Don't lie about your GPA!

- Be honest and accurate.

- Don't round off your GPA.

- Don't include your GPA for your major only. This communicates that your overall GPA was lower.

<u>Cover Letters</u>: A cover letter shows you went the extra mile. Here you can expand on your accomplishments. A cover letter also allows the opportunity to show off your writing skills. A well-written cover letter can move your résumé to the top of the pile.

That's it on résumés. I hope, reading this chapter will help you land a pharmaceuticals sales job. Once you land it, you want to succeed in it. Read on, because it's not over yet. Learn how to do the job right!

Chapter Two

What It Takes

"Nothing in the world can take the place of persistence. Talent will not. Nothing is more common than unsuccessful men with talent. Genius will not. Unrewarded genius is almost the proverb. Education will not. The world is full of educated derelicts. Persistence, determination and hard work make a difference."
—President Calvin Coolidge

THE FOUR GUIDING PRINCIPLES

This was one of the first slides my first regional sales director presented when I was a rep and I have never forgotten it. He presented this slide during every POA meeting. I have been presenting this slide to salespeople and managers as a district manager and now as a national sales director. You should never forget the lessons and tools you learned during your career, especially if you think they have contributed to your success.

Four Guiding Principles for Success

Positive Attitude   **Hard Work**

Success!

Execute the Fundamentals

Integrity

When I present this slide either at a POA meeting or to a new training class, I tell them that they need to embrace all four principles to succeed. If one is missing, it will be difficult to succeed. Let's first address each principle then I'll explain why you need to embrace all four in order to succeed.

Positive Attitude

When you wake up in the morning you get to do something that no other person in the world can take away from you, not your boss, competition, or even your spouse. It's your freedom to *choose your attitude!* You get to choose whether you are going to have a great day or a bad day. The hardest thing to do is to maintain a positive attitude when you are having a bad day. I can't think of anything more difficult to do. Those few salespeople that do it are usually the most successful. Choosing your attitude means when you are having a bad day and normally allow it to affect the way you do your job, but then choose not to allow it to happen. Instead, you pick yourself up and do your job.

When you are having a bad day, think about what you

love most about your job, what you love about people, and what people love about you. Think about the smiles you see when you walk into an office and when the office staff calls you by name (like Norm in Cheers). You go on with your day, continue to make your calls, and you congratulate yourself for changing your attitude and making a difference.

When I first became a district manager, the trainers would coach us not to mention the word "attitude." They would say that you can't change a person's attitude. I never believed that. I had no problem telling reps that they needed to change their attitudes or in some extreme cases I would say, "your attitude stinks!"

It's easy to forget and take for granted how good you have it. As a pharmaceutical salesperson you earn more money than most people in this country. You get to interact in a social setting with office staff and engage doctors in professional discussions. You learn and get to make a difference in people's lives. Whether it's cheering up the receptionist who's having a bad day or providing the doctor medicines that help heal people.

Don't Complain!

Since you will be interacting with people daily, you will need to be "On" every day. The last thing a doctor and staff need is another person moping around their office complaining about their jobs. They see sick patients all day with complaints. Also, don't complain to your manager.

As with any job, things won't always go as planned. In pharmaceutical sales, your sample shipment may not arrive on time; a managed care company could pull your product from its formulary; your computer often will not cooperate; the help desk will often prove to be helpless. Whatever the problem, resist the urge to complain. Instead, solve your problems and do your job!

Work Ethic:

As I mentioned in Chapter One, a strong work ethic means different things to different people. In order to succeed in pharmaceutical sales, you need to want to be a hard worker. You got to love the job. Working from nine to five might make you an average rep. Working late doing dinner programs, working early in the emergency room, seeking out doctors with early and late office hours, and making many calls every day will make you an above average rep. To be exceptional, you got to have it all: work ethic, product knowledge, great personality and relationships, and solid selling skills.

Integrity

"Tell the truth. That way you don't have to make up a story."
John Wooden (Famous UCLA basketball coach)

During one of my first business management courses in college, I remember the professor saying that the Ethics chapter of our management book was the most important. I also remember it being one of the longest and most boring. I never took that chapter or discussion seriously. I had thought it was a bunch of fluff until when I had read about the Enron and WorldCom executives and their blatant disregard for integrity.

There is much temptation in this job to cut corners and break the rules. Some reps steal money off the expense report. Some break guidelines set by the pharmaceutical industry by buying doctors gifts. Doctors may even ask you do something that would be breaking the rules. If you are ever in a situation when you have to ask yourself whether you should or shouldn't do something, then play it safe and don't do it. When I would find myself in these situations, I would always ask myself if it something that I would want my own child to do or would my parents be proud of me if I did it.

If a doctor asks you to do something that you know is not the right thing to do, then don't do it. There are many other doctors in your territory that can help drive your business. Even if they are the "whale" it is not worth losing your job and integrity.

THE FUNDAMENTALS

I dedicated Chapter Three to the Five Fundamentals of the job. In any profession, there are fundamentals that you will need to execute to be successful. In football, players need to tackle, block, and run. In baseball, batters need to hit, fielders need to catch a ball. In basketball, players need to dribble, shoot and pass a ball. The best athletes practice these fundamentals every day. The best hitters in baseball take extra batting practice, the best basketball players shoot more free throws during and after practice. Michael Jordan did not make his high school basketball team as a sophomore. He needed to work hard, and practice to play as a junior.

In pharmaceutical sales, some of those fundamentals include calling on the right doctors, planning calls, delivering a product message, using visual aids, and asking for the business. This requires a lot of studying, practice, and dedicating your free time to perfect your skills, just like an athlete.

Rodney Dangerfield & The Real World

An instructor of one of my MBA courses was the Executive Director of Business Development for Merck's veterinary division. He presented textbook information about drug marketing with little understanding of how pharmaceutical companies promoted drugs to doctors. Knowing that I was the only pharmaceutical salesperson in the class made him nervous. During discussions about marketing to doctors, he would seek my approval. I would throw in my two cents—I couldn't help myself. I felt like Rodney Dangerfield in the movie *Back To School*: When the business professor would discuss textbook examples of widgets and production costs, Rodney Dangerfield would constantly interrupt the nerdy professor and offer his real-life business experience. The students would then face Rodney and start taking notes—it's a hysterical scene!

During one my classes, the professor slammed the chalkboard with what he thought were the most important parts of pharmaceutical sales:

- Breaking the ice before discussing products

- Building a relationship with the doctor

- Establishing credibility

- Delivering the marketing message

When he was through abusing the chalkboard, he whirled around, faced me, and awaited my approval.

"You're missing one," I said. He was missing more than just one, but I gave him a break. "Closing the sale!" I explained. "You can do a great job of breaking the ice, building the best relationships in the world, establishing credibility by knowing your products, and delivering the right marketing message, but if you don't ask for the business, you won't get it!"

In Mark McCormack's book, *What They Still Don't Teach You At Harvard Business School*, McCormack provides the following characteristics of a successful salesperson:

- Know your product
- See a lot of people
- Ask all to buy
- Use common sense

KNOW YOUR PRODUCTS

"You have to know the competition as well."
—Mark McCormack

"Understand how your product is used so you can understand how to sell it most effectively."
—*The Sales Bible*, Jeffrey H. Gitomer

Take extra time to study your products. Not embarrassing myself was always a great incentive for me. If a doctor asks a question about your product, it works to your advantage to know the answer. When you don't know the answer, it's sometimes acceptable to get back to the doctor during your next visit. This can help show your reliability, but it's not OK when you consistently do not know the most basic things about your products. The more often you have to get back to a doctor with an answer, the more credibility you lose. Most of the time, the answers are in the package insert or on the visual aids. Study and learn something new about your products every day.

Learn Something New Every Day

- Keep a Product Notebook

- Read the Studies

- Understand Everything on your Promotional Pieces and Visual Aids

- Read the Package Insert while Waiting in Offices

Going to training and scoring hundreds on your tests are not enough. Take about twenty to thirty minutes each day to read and learn something about your products. Keep a product notebook. When you learn something new, record it in your notebook and be sure to revisit it. Sometimes, when a doctor asked a question, I would whip out my little notebook and provide the answer. That impressed them. They knew I took pride in my job.

During educational speaker programs, take notes and learn something. Don't just sit there and eat. Listen up! The speaker will discuss your drugs and disease states that your drugs treat, and your doctors may ask questions. This provides you with an excellent opportunity to follow up with your doctors who asked questions. During your follow up visit (which should be the next day) you could say something like, "Hey, Dr. Smith, I noticed you asked a question about drug interactions during the program. I just wanted to show you this list of drugs that Drug X does not interact with."

Read and understand the major studies that your company provides. Often a doctor may ask details about a study, such as the number of patients, demographics, disease states, doses, and other information. Keep a product notebook with notes on all the studies your company provides.

Understand everything on the visual aids, so when you mention something about them to your doctors, you know what you are talking about. You should know every word, graph, and footnote. For example, if you are showing a graph on your visual aid that shows your product performed better than another product, then you should know which study and the drugs used in the graph. You should also know both the generic and branded names of the products in the study.

During a sales call with one of my reps, the doctor had asked the rep if we had any studies comparing our drug to the most popular drug in the same class. When the salesperson said, "I'll get back to you on that," I was mystified.

When we left the doctor's office, I asked the salesperson if we had any information in our visual aid that compared our drug to the drug mentioned by the doctor. He insisted that we did not. I told him to open the visual aid—the same visual aid he had been using for the last six months! I pointed to where our drug was compared to the other drug. Because the visual aid showed the generic name of the other drug and the doctor had used the brand name, the rep hadn't been able to identify the drug. I said, "You mean to tell me that for the last six months, you have been selling this drug showing doctors this visual aid on how our drug compares with the most popular drug in the world, and you don't even know the brand name?" Unbelievable!

The visual aids also include disease states that you should know. For example, one visual aid showed that our drug was indicated for patients who have suffered an MI or TIA. Would you believe that some salespeople mention these terms to doctors and do not know what they mean? If you don't know what they mean, have the foresight to look it up!

While you are waiting to see the doctor, read the package insert (PI) instead of *People Magazine*. It is impossible to know everything on the PI. If the doctor asks a question about your product and you don't know the answer, you should at least know where in the PI to find it.

ACTIVITY=RESULTS!

See a Lot of People

I have always said that *Activity = Results!* The more doctors you see and sell to, the more sales you will make. The most successful reps are usually the ones who make the most calls. Sales reps could easily make ten or more calls a day. Poor performing or even average reps usually make excuses for making fewer than 10 calls per day. You can see doctors early in hospitals, late in clinics. You can figure out which doctors start office hours early and those who end late. If you have great relationships with the staff and doctors, they won't mind seeing you early in the morning or late in the evening. Rather, they will expect to see you. (*See Fundamental 1: Targeting and Planning in Chapter Three.*)

DO A LOT OF DINNER Programs

Doing dinner programs has become more difficult than before with new industry and company guidelines. Reps constantly invite doctors to programs that often do not want to attend. But even with the new restrictions and competition from other companies, the best reps are still able to get doctors out to programs. Many reps use the restrictions as excuses not to do the programs. The truth is they don't want to take time from their personal lives and they don't have the relationships. Doctors attend the programs because they like the rep. They know which reps are dedicated, genuine and with which reps they would enjoy spending their free time.

During dinner programs, work on developing your

relationships with your doctors and let the speaker take care of the educational part. This is not the time to sell your products. Sell while you are in their offices or in the hospitals. You will find that doctors who normally did not give you much time to sell in the office will be more receptive to your selling efforts after attending a dinner program. The relationship that you build during dinner programs will earn you more time to sell during your office visits.

There's something about breaking bread and having a glass of wine with people that improves your relationship with them to a different level.

Another goal of a dinner program is for the speaker to engage other doctors in your territory in a discussion about the indications of your drug and how to use it in specific patient types. If your product provides features, benefits and advantages over other drugs, the speaker can communicate that during the program. For the speaker to effectively discuss the benefits of your drug over others, he should have clinical experience using your drug.

Dinner programs can also help doctors build their practices. If the speaker is a specialist in a particular field and respected by other doctors based on their knowledge and presentation skills, they can earn referrals from other doctors. This makes you a valuable resource for the speaker and your other doctors present.

The environment of these programs has changed from a formal setting using a projector and screen to more informal round-table discussion. This allows for a more intimate setting and more conversation between the speaker and your doctors.

The size of the audience and the speaker's preference will decide whether a program will be a round-table discussion or a stand-up presentation with all the bells and whistles. If there are five or fewer doctors, then a round-table setting would be more appropriate than a stand-up presentation. For a larger audience, using slides, projector and screen may work better. You may find that doctors in your territory prefer small round-table discussions rather than larger programs. Be sure to work out the details with the speaker and your audience before the program

I enjoyed watching my reps help their speakers prepare the slide presentations. This allowed the speakers and my reps to work as a team and build solid relationships (see Appendix 3 for a checklist for Successful Educational Dinner Programs).

The more dinner programs you do, the better relationships you will build. You will gain better access and doctors will learn more about your drugs and how to use them. As a result, doctors will use your products more often and you will improve your sales performance.

Analyze Yourself and Your Business

Think about and evaluate your business. Do you do the same thing every day and not see any difference in your sales results and continue to do the same things? We call this insanity! Are you calling on your top docs? Are they giving you a fair share of the business? If not, what are you going to do to change the situation? Are you delivering solid presentations? Are you closing after every call? After you make a call, do you ask yourself whether you sold anything?

Analyze your numbers, your call frequency and yourself. If you are not thinking about your business and how to improve it every day, then it is time for a new career that does not require thinking!

Every rep should prepare and present a business plan to their manager. That means preparing about 10 PowerPoint Slides that include:

- Where You Are

- Where You Want to Be

- How Are You Going to Get There

As a district manager, I had my reps prepare and present a business plan that answers these questions. I provided the template on PowerPoint, and then presented their plans in front of the Team. Now as a sales director, I have my managers and reps do the same.

Where You Are:
- Your overall sales performance for the most recent year separated by quarter. Most companies provide ranking reports that rank you versus other reps in your region or nationally.

- Your sales performance by product. This can include your rank, market share, market share change, volume, or volume change. It depends on how your company evaluates your performance.

- Activity: Remember, Activity=Results! You should know and evaluate the following activity quarterly:
  - *call average*
  - *number of calls*
  - *dinner programs*
  - *lunches/breakfasts*

Where You Want to Be:
Set some short and long-term goals for yourself based on your current performance. You may want to rank #3 in your district or region by the next quarter and # 1 by the end of the year. Be sure your goals are specific and realistic. If your goal is to win President's Club,

then your current ranking will need to be in the top 10%. Assign a specific time period for your goals.

How Are You Going to Get There:

This is the essence of your business plan, where you plan specific action steps of what you are going to do moving forward. Once again, set specific action plans with assigned dates. Here are some examples:

- Increase calls on my top 5 doctors from twice a month to 4 times a month.

- Redo my 2-week schedule to reflect the increase in call frequency. Complete schedule by December 20th and start calling on these doctors every week starting Jan 2nd.

- Schedule a dinner program with Dr. Smith.

- Visit him Monday Jan 8th for a Jan 25th dinner program.

- Ask Dr. Jones if he would be available on Jan 25th to speak.

- Make an appointment with the director of pharmacy at Saint Mary's Hospital.
  - *Call director Tues Jan 11th*
  - *Schedule lunch for Wed Jan 12th*

The most important part of your business plan is that you go out and execute your plan with the goal of driving your business. When you write things down and set dates, there is much better chance of getting things done rather than just winging it.

Developing and presenting a business plan will not only help you drive your business, but will also improve the following skills:

- PowerPoint and Excel

- Presentation Skills

- Analytical Skills

- Planning and Organization

Develop Yourself

Don't just rely on training and your manager for your development. Your goal should be to develop yourself into the best possible salesperson. That means consistently practicing your presentations and investing twenty to thirty minutes a day to increase your product knowledge. Here are some other action items you can do as part of your continuous improvement plan:

- Read Books: Try to read one book a month. (See Appendix 2 for some of my favorites.)

- Dale Carnegie Training: Most pharmaceutical companies will reimburse you anywhere from 80 to 100% of the cost of any courses you want to take. Take advantage of this perk and register for a Dale Carnegie course. I send my managers and reps to courses such as "High Impact Presentations," "Developing an Executive Image," and "Influencing People." Check out the website for a course listing: www.dalecarnegie.com.

- Franklin Covey Training: As well as offering the

course, "The 7 Habits of Highly Successful People."
Other courses are available on how to get organized
using a planner or palm pilot. Check out the
website: www.franklincovey.com.

Get Organized

You cannot do this job without a planner. You should
either have a Franklin Planner, a Palm Pilot or something
equivalent. You need to schedule lunches, appointments,
dinner programs, sales meetings, birthdays, and other
events. You also need to have a To-Do List—there will be
plenty to do!

Prioritize your To-Do List. Write a letter or number next
to your To-Do item, in order of importance. For example, if
you have five things on your list and the most important one
is to call your manager, then place an "A" or a "1" next to it.
The next most important item will be either "B" or "2".

During and after each field visit with my reps, I assigned
tasks and follow-up items. When they just stared at me
instead of writing things down, as if they were going to
remember everything I had just said, that's when I would say,
"Are you going to write this down?"

I highly suggest using a Palm Pilot or the new Palm
phones. Planners can be cumbersome to carry along with
samples, product binder, promotional items, and anything
else you need to take with you into a doctor's office. With a
Palm Pilot, as soon as you get a business card, you can immediately input the names, addresses and phone numbers
of your doctors and office staff. Palms also have programs
that allow you to input events and other information, such
as birthdays. You can download programs from the Internet
such as *epocrates*, which include all current drugs on the
market. And best of all, you can back up your information on

a PC or laptop. If you lose your regular planner, you lose all that information—with a Palm, it's all backed up.

Most important, bring your planner or Palm into the office. Would you believe that some reps try to schedule events with doctors without their planner? I have seen reps try to schedule a lunch without their planner not knowing that they might have another lunch or event scheduled for that day.

Keep well-organized product folders in your car. Some reps use milk crates as their filing cabinets. Separate your product literature with tabs, labeling different studies for each product. Include extra selling aids as well. Also keep similar folders in your storage unit so you can easily refill the files you keep in your car. And lastly, keep a well-organized product binder to bring into the office. Be sure to use fresh pieces—showing a doctor a worn detail piece looks unprofessional. People who do that are the same ones who might present a résumé covered with coffee stains.

Develop a Sense of Humor

A doctor once told me that his attention span was no more than ten seconds. He was a tiny, frail, Indian doctor who spoke so softly and with such an accent that I had to position my ear close to his mouth to understand him. I learned from another rep that he loved telling jokes. I didn't believe it! During my next visit, I asked him to tell me a joke. I had never seen him light up like that. He told me a joke that really made me laugh and then told me to come back next week and he would tell me another joke. Can you imagine—a doctor who tells you to come back just to tell you a joke?

I went back the following week, not only prepared to hear another joke, but with one of my own. I spent about five minutes with him exchanging jokes and another five minutes discussing my products. His attention span went from ten seconds to ten minutes!

The point is that if you don't have a sense of humor, develop one and use it to sell. I was never known to have a good sense of humor. As a matter of fact, most people told me that I was too serious. But I have loosened up. I owe some of my newly found humor to Howard Stern. You would be surprised to learn how many doctors listen to Howard Stern.

However, having a great sense of humor won't do you much good if you don't sell. You can learn to transition the joke to your product. Or simply ask the doctor if he has another minute to discuss one product point.

Be Nice

In grade school, I remember one of my teachers would always tell the students not to use the word "nice" because people overused it. But in pharmaceutical sales, you really do have to be nice. Be nice to everyone. Be nice to the people in elevators, on line in the bank, or at the supermarket. You never know whom you might meet. If you are working in a hospital, chances are there will be plenty of doctors and nurses in the elevator. Be nice to the janitors, the parking attendants, the office staff, the patients—anyone you meet during your day.

During this book, I discuss the importance of the basic fundamentals of the job such as delivering sales messages and planning calls. In order to succeed in this business, doctors and office staff need to like you, regardless of your selling skills. It's true that people buy from people they like.

I recommend you read *How to Win Friends and Influence People,* by Dale Carnegie. The key is not just to be nice, but to be genuinely nice. People can tell when you are being genuine or fake. Make an effort every day to compliment someone on their appearance. Think about the last time you wore a new blouse, suit, tie, or shoes, and wondered if anyone noticed. Even though no one may have complimented you on your new pair of shoes, someone may have been thinking it, but just didn't say it. Think about the last time you were in this situation. You can make someone's day with a simple compliment.

Don't Be a Slob

Let's face it, it's true what they say about a first impression— it may be your last. I couldn't help but laugh at reps with shirts sticking out of their pants, flies open, stained shirts and ties, torn shoes, and ill-fitting suits. Doctors take notice of what you wear and how you present yourself to them. They appreciate a professional look. Men should wear suits. That means wearing the jacket, regardless of the weather. Women should not wear mini skirts and clothing that exposes tattoos. I have nothing against tattoos, but doctors don't need to see them.

During my interview process for my first pharmaceutical sales position, I conducted a telephone interview with a doctor. When I asked him what he looked for in a salesperson, the first thing he mentioned was appearance. He told me about a rep that used to call on him. He laughed as he reminisced about the rep's greasy hair pressed down on his forehead; his fat stomach that bulged out of his coffee-stained shirt, revealing his undershirt and bellybutton hairs. His suit, when he did wear a jacket, looked as if he had just pulled it out of the laundry basket. The doctor roared on the other end of the phone as he told me the story and I roared with him. He added that no other doctor in the office would see the rep. He had agreed to see the rep only because he was so fascinated by the man's sloppiness. Trust me—this is not how you want doctors to remember you.

GO THE EXTRA MILE!

This can simply mean bringing coffee and doughnuts to an office. Some reps bring the doughnuts without the coffee. Dunkin Donuts offers the Box-O-Joe, and Starbucks something similar. A box of coffee serves about ten cups of coffee. You may have to wait several minutes in long lines, and the customers behind you may start grumbling, but that's what I mean about going the extra mile. The office staff will appreciate the coffee and it usually earns you extra time with the doctor. So don't be lazy; get the coffee.

During one of my attempts to go above and beyond, I offered to hang a huge picture frame on the newly painted walls in a doctor's reception room. At first, the office manager asked me if I had any tools that she could use to hang up some pictures. They were cheap-looking prints. The one I was going to hang was a painting of a tree, mountain landscape, and a river—exciting! You would have thought from the size of the frame that I was hanging a Van-Gogh.

When I told her that I had a toolbox in my car, she handed me these huge screws. The last time I had tried hanging anything in my place resulted in my ceiling looking like Swiss cheese—nothing a little toothpaste couldn't cover. Those holes were nothing compared to the ones I made in the doctor's wall! It looked like a mouse had bored right through the sheet rock. The problem was that I kept hitting a beam—the thick screws would not penetrate deeply enough to hold the painting.

As I worked, I realized that I was providing entertainment for the patients in the waiting room. For the first time ever, they didn't seem to mind waiting to see the doctor. They were watching a guy in a suit, with sweat dripping down his face, trying desperately to hang a picture on a wall. I was covered with sheet rock residue and looked as if I had just struggled through an algebra problem on a chalkboard.

After about a half hour of embarrassing myself, I finally decided to go to the nearest hardware store. I bought the right nails and two hours later completed the job. The result was the doctor appreciated it (I don't think my manager would have) and it earned me more time to sell.

Don't Be A Loser!

Some reps turn to alternative measures to selling —begging. I remember a rep that was notorious for his off-the-wall antics, such as discarding other reps' samples. He would also beg and use the sympathy approach to selling. During a discussion with one of the office managers, I discovered that this rep was telling the doctor about his marriage plans and house hunting. He begged the doctor to increase prescriptions for his drug so he could pay for his wedding and house. The office manager told me the doctor felt sorry for the rep. What a loser!

Whether this worked or not, don't be a loser. Don't use the line that you are going to get fired if your sales don't increase. Doctors don't want to hear it. They are not practicing medicine for you. They will think you are a big loser. Doctors prefer to see reps with good attitudes and upbeat personalities.

One rep claimed that he had prostate cancer. One of the doctor investigated his story and learned it was a lie. The doctor and the office staff never confronted the rep about the lie, but told me the rep was still coming in and talking about his prostate cancer—loser!

Another rep was car-jacked and robbed at gunpoint outside one of the busiest offices in my territory. The office staff and other reps told me the rep took full advantage of the incident by reminding the doctor how he'd almost gotten killed and that, therefore, the doctor should write more prescriptions for his products—loser!

Chapter Three

The Five Fundamentals

I can still picture my first district manager's head—
inches away from mine as we sat in the car during pre-call
planning, barking in my face and dropping f-bombs: "You
better be following the Five Fundamentals, I f___n mean it!"
He drilled me on the Five Fundamentals from the first day
he interviewed me until the last day we rode together. He
quizzed me on them until I could rattle them off. He made
me tape them to my steering wheel until finally, I said, "OK, I
believe in them—really. I'm sold."

My first manager was an exceptional salesperson and sold
me on the Five Fundamentals. As a district manager and now
a national sales director, I continue to sell managers and reps
to follow them (minus the barking and f-bombs). I evaluate
and determine salary increases based on how my managers
coach and how the reps execute the Five Fundamentals.

1. Targeting and Planning
2. Pre-Call Planning and Post-Call Analysis
3. Effective Use of Literature
4. Following the Plan of Action (POA)
5. Closing (Asking for the Business)

FUNDAMENTAL 1: TARGETING AND PLANNING

This entails seeing the right doctors, the right amount of times, at the right times. The right doctors are the ones who write the most prescriptions for a particular drug class. The right number of times means seeing the right doctors anywhere from two to four times per month or more. And the right time means early in the week and when they maybe most accessible.

Now that most pharmaceutical companies are moving away from Pods or several reps calling call on the same doctors, it's even more important to increase the frequency on top doctors than before.

The 80/20 Rule

The 80/20 Rule says that 80% of your business will come from 20% of your customers. In this business, that means 80% of all the prescriptions written for your product in your territory will come from about 20% of your doctors. Large territories with 1000 or more doctors make it difficult to call on the top 20% two to four times per month. That would be an average of 600 calls per month. That's why some companies pay salespeople based only on the top 100 doctors in each territory. That's why you mainly focus on the top doctors in your territory.

Even if your company pays you on the prescribing habits of all 100 doctors, it still does not mean that you have to see all 100 doctors. Concentrate on the top 50. I have always believed on calling on fewer top doctors with high frequency rather than many doctors with low frequency. People still argue with me that the way to go is to call on many doctors, but I continue to prove them wrong every time. It is difficult to build relationships and change prescribing habits of top doctors with only one visit per month.

Also, the number one and two doctors in your territory may collectively generate more prescriptions than the next 10 doctors on your list. Getting the top 25 doctors in your territory to prescribe 20-30% percent of your drug is better than getting 50 doctors ranked 50-100 to prescribe 50-60% of your drug.

Let's say your manager tells you to focus on the top 30 doctors for one product. Then call on the top 15 doctors four times per month and the next 15 (16-30), two times per month—that's 180 calls per month. Some doctors who write many prescriptions for several drug classes (we call them "super doctors") can be called on five or more times per month, especially if they have more than one office.

The number of drugs you sell will also determine the number of doctors and the number of times you will call on each of them. Successful reps make more than 200 calls per month or 10 or more calls per day. Some reps average 11-13 calls per day. I always tell them to be sure that most of those calls are on target doctors. I'm not interested in them calling on doctors way down on the list that are unlikely to drive their sales.

I am also not interested in reps making 13 sample-drops a day. That means saying hello to the doctor, leaving samples, getting a signature and out the door they go—no selling at all. No way! I always tell them that I can hire a UPS person to do that for $30,000 a year. Be sure you make an impact and sell something on every call.

New reps sometimes get into a bad habit of calling on too many doctors. When I first started, I made this mistake. I would stop my car every time I saw a doctor's office. It took me a long time to embrace the 80/20 Rule. I thought the more doctors I saw, the more prescriptions I would generate. I was wrong. There is a difference between making a lot of doctor calls and seeing a lot of doctors. The key is to see the top doctors frequently, not to make infrequent calls on a lot of different doctors.

New reps also make the mistake of calling on doctors who are easy to see. The easy-to-see doctors usually give you time because they have the time. If they have all that time to spend with you, that means they are not seeing many patients, which means they are not writing a lot of prescriptions. The doctors who are difficult to see are usually the ones who are writing most of the prescriptions—the ones you need to drive your business.

Time and resources are limited. The average doctor-call costs a company about $200! This does not even include the cost of samples, food, parking, and other costs. If it costs your company $200 per office visit and the doctor only writes 10 total prescriptions in a month for that drug class, then there is no possible "return on investment." Get used to that term, because you will be hearing it a lot from your manager. You will also want to use your lunch budget and promotional items, such as pens and pads, on the top doctors' offices. You will not have enough resources to allocate to 200 doctors.

Trackers

A tracker is a list of doctors you plan to call on for each product (*see next page*). A well-organized tracker shows the doctor's product rank, the number of times you plan to call on that doctor in a month, and the actual number of times you called on that doctor during that month. This ensures the right frequency.

In the example on the next page, Dr. Smith is ranked number 1, based on the number of prescriptions he writes in that drug class. The plan is to see him four times a month.

The last column shows the percentage of actual calls to planned calls. Of course, I would like to see 100% of calls made, but it doesn't always work out that way. Since it is difficult to make 100% of the planned calls, the goal would be to make at least 80% of the calls. It's most important to make the calls on the top 10 to 15 doctors. In the example below, I will be asking questions about why Dr. Gold, the third-ranked doctor, was only seen once during the month.

Tracker: Product A

Rank	Doctor	Planned Calls	Actual Calls Made	% of Calls Made
1	Smith	4	3	75%
2	Jones	4	5	125%
3	Gold	4	1	25%
4	Red	4	4	100%
.				
.				
.				
16	Orange	2	2	100%
17	Silver	2	0	0%

I provide my sales reps with Excel spreadsheets that are much more detailed than my handwritten version. They include formulas to calculate the percentage of calls made on the top 15 doctors, as well as the percentage of total calls made compared to the planned calls.

If you sell more than one product, you should have a tracker for each product. Super doctors should appear on only one tracker. If a doctor shows up on more than one tracker the calls will be counted on all trackers inflating the number of calls made. Reps should include a super doctor on the tracker where the doctor is more important to their business.

The 2-Week Schedule

The 2-Week Schedule should include all doctors who are on your tracker(s). Although we call it a 2-Week Schedule, it is actually a monthly schedule, because Week 1 should be the same as Week 3 and Week 2 the same as Week 4. For example, the 2-Week schedule on the next page shows that Drs. Smith and Jones are listed in Week 1 & 2, which means every Monday of the month. If you plan to see a doctor only twice a month, then that doctor should be listed only once on the 2-Week Schedule. In the example, Drs. Orange and Silver will be seen on the first and third Tuesday of each month because Week 1 is the same as Week 3.

You should plan to call on a doctor either twice or four times per month. This adds consistency to your scheduling calling on the same doctors on the same days. This also helps construct an organized 2-Week Schedule rather than a 3-Week or Monthly schedule. You shouldn't plan to call on a doctor once per month, because as I mentioned before, it is difficult develop relationships and drive business with only one call per month.

The most important doctors should be seen early in the

week—every Monday or Tuesday—so that when they write prescriptions for your drugs on Monday or Tuesday, they will continue writing for them throughout the week. The reason why you wouldn't want to wait to see a top doctor on a Friday, is because when Monday rolls around, the doctor may have forgotten about your visit. If Friday is the only day when you can see that doctor, then try to see him early in the day. It's important to follow a consistent schedule. That means seeing the same doctors on the same days and times during the month to ensure the right frequency on the top doctors.

The 2-Week Schedule includes the following to help you plan your month, week, day, and calls:

- Doctor's name

- Specialty

- Rank for each product

- Office hours

- Add-ins

THE 2-WEEK SCHEDULE

Week One	MONDAY	Specialty	Hours	Prod A Rank	Prod B Rank	TUESDAY	Specialty	Hours	Prod A Rank	Prod B Rank	WEDNESDAY	Specialty	Hours	Prod A Rank	Prod B Rank	THURSDAY	Specialty	Hours	Prod A Rank	Prod B Rank	FRIDAY	Specialty	Hours	Prod A Rank
1	Dr. Smith	IM	8-5	1	9	Dr. Gold	IM	8:30-12	2	124	Doctor's Name	MEP	8-3	15	17	Doctor's Name	IM	8-4	33	62	Doctor's Name	IM	8-4	53
2	Dr. Jones	CD	9-5	4	16	Dr. Red	END	8:30-12	5	11	Doctor's Name	GE	8-4	39	437	Doctor's Name	IM	8-5	32	36	Doctor's Name	IM	8-4	405
3	Dr. Pharma	IM	10-1	1	69	Dr. Apple	IM	10:30-3	7	37	Doctor's Name	OC	8-4	49	347	Doctor's Name	CD	8-4	79	332	Doctor's Name	CD	8-4	72
4	Dr. Drug	IM	9-5	13	150	Dr. Orange	CD	9-12	27	502	Doctor's Name	CD	10-4	99	19	Doctor's Name	CD	8-4	27	293	Doctor's Name	CD	8-4	27
5	Dr. Computer	IM	12-6	30	123	Dr. Silver	GE	10-3	34	415	Doctor's Name	CD	12-4	84	45	Doctor's Name	IM	8-4	130	63	Doctor's Name	RE	8-4	130
6	Dr. Printer	IM	11-4	11	1	Dr. Black	IM	9:00-12:00	10	187	Doctor's Name	CD	8-5	253	73	Doctor's Name	IM	8-5	119	64	Doctor's Name	IM	8-5	113
7	Dr. Desk	IM	9-5	118	2	Dr. Yellow	NEP	9:30-3:00	12	34	Doctor's Name	IM	9-6	602	16	Doctor's Name	GE	8-5	29	229	Doctor's Name	IM	8-5	24
8	Dr. Chair	IM	10-7	417	3	Dr. Green	GE	9:00-4:00	14	84	Doctor's Name	IM	11-7	77	33	Doctor's Name	IM	8-5	80	64	Doctor's Name	IM	8-5	95
9	Dr. Key	ONC	11-8	36	8	Dr. Magenta	GE	9:00-5:00	15	84	Doctor's Name	IM	13-7	0	90	Doctor's Name	ELEC	8-5	70	82	Doctor's Name	IM	8-4	78
10	Dr. Wire	GE	11-8	340	4	Dr. Seven	IM	10:30-5:00	16	22	Doctor's Name	IM	9-7	14	33	Doctor's Name	IM	8-4	127	29	Doctor's Name	RNE	8-4	137
	Add-ins					Add-ins					Add-ins					Add-ins					Add-ins			
	Add-ins					Add-ins					Add-ins					Add-ins					Add-ins			
	Add-ins					Add-ins					Add-ins					Add-ins					Add-ins			

Week Two		Specialty	Hours	Prod A Rank	Prod B Rank		Specialty	Hours	Prod A Rank	Prod B Rank		Specialty	Hours	Prod A Rank	Prod B Rank		Specialty	Hours	Prod A Rank	Prod B Rank		Specialty	Hours	Prod A Rank
1	Dr. Smith	CD	8-5	7	9	Dr. Gold	IM	8-5	2	11	Doctor's Name	IM	8-4	39	427	Doctor's Name	IM	8-4	33	84	Doctor's Name	IM	8-4	33
2	Dr. Jones	IM	8-7	4	76	Dr. Red	END	8-7	6	37	Doctor's Name	IM	8-5	88	495	Doctor's Name	IM	8-4	495	34	Doctor's Name	IM	8-4	17
3	Dr. Pharma	IM	10-4	1	69	Dr. Apple	IM	10-4	7	602	Doctor's Name	IM	8-5	30	542	Doctor's Name	CD	8-5	79	332	Doctor's Name	IM	8-6	12
4	Dr. Drug	IM	9:30-5	13	158	Dr. Sleep	CD	9:30-5	27	615	Doctor's Name	IM	8-4	61	401	Doctor's Name	CD	8-4	27	293	Doctor's Name	IM	8-4	36
5	Dr. Computer	IM	12-6	30	196	Dr. Fall	GE	12-6	34	167	Doctor's Name	IM	8-4	64	259	Doctor's Name	CD	8-4	130	63	Doctor's Name	IM	8-4	66
6	Dr. Printer	IM	12-6	11	1	Dr. Mauve	IM	12-6	10	167	Doctor's Name	IM	8-4	641	87	Doctor's Name	IM	8-5	119	45	Doctor's Name	IM	8-5	76
7	Dr. Desk	IM	12-6	118	2	Dr. Yellow	NEP	12-6	12	84	Doctor's Name	IM	9-6	40	565	Doctor's Name	GE	8-5	78	229	Doctor's Name	IM	8-4	71
8	Dr. Chair	ONC	12-6	417	3	Dr. Green	GE	12-6	14	23	Doctor's Name	ENO	9-6	114	33	Doctor's Name	IM	8-4	67	229	Doctor's Name	IM	8-4	67
9	Dr. Key	OE	12-6	36	9	Dr. Magenta	GE	12-6	16	22	Doctor's Name	IV	8-6	9	29	Doctor's Name	ELEC	8-4	24	648	Doctor's Name	IM	8-4	74
10	Dr. Wire	CD	8-7	340	4	Dr. Seven	IM	2-7	16	75	Doctor's Name	IV	8-6	22	483	Doctor's Name	IM	8-6	62	239	Doctor's Name	CD	8-4	92
	Add-ins					Add-ins					Add-ins					Add-ins					Add-ins			
	Add-ins					Add-ins					Add-ins					Add-ins					Add-ins			
	Add-ins					Add-ins					Add-ins					Add-ins					Add-ins			

This 2-Week Schedule shows 10 doctors to be seen each day for a total of 200 calls per month. Notice the doctors' ranks, specialties and office hours. The rank shows the importance of the doctor. Knowing the doctor's specialty allows you to tailor the presentation to that type of doctor. Your presentation to a cardiologist may be different from the one you make to an internal medicine doctor. The office hours on the 2-Week Schedule will avoid trying to visit a doctor that does not have office hours during that time (not something you want to do when you are with your manager).

Add-ins

Add-in doctors could be non-target doctors or doctors low on a call list (they may be ranked 60 through 80 for a particular drug class) that may have some potential or may have written a few prescriptions for your products. I coach my reps to include add-in doctors on their trackers and 2-Week Schedules for the following reasons:

- A rep did not make the required 10 target calls during the day and has time to visit other doctors.

- The non-target doctor's office is near or in the same building as a target office.

- The rep made the required 10 target calls and wants to make more calls.

- The doctor is a specialist, such as a cardiologist or endocrinologist.

- The doctor is head of a department in a local hospital and has influence over other doctors or at a hospital.

- The doctor writes a respectable number of prescriptions for more than one drug. Although a doctor may not be a target for any one product, the sum of the prescriptions the doctor writes for several drug classes makes him worth calling on.

Daily Schedule

From your 2-Week Schedule, make a daily schedule because, let's face it, things don't always go as planned. There are many things that can change the 2-Week Schedule, such as meetings, holidays and vacations. Your 2-Week Schedule is not written in stone—it is simply a map of all your doctors and when you will usually see them. Your daily schedule will determine where you will be every day. For example, if Dr. Smith who was scheduled for Monday was on vacation, then see him on Tuesday if he is back from vacation. You would not want to wait until the following Monday to see him, because you could lose an entire week of prescriptions. Also, let's say you see Dr. Smith on Monday and it's his birthday on Friday; then you would deviate from your 2-Week Schedule and see him both days to wish him a happy birthday on Friday. Take a few minutes in the morning to plan your day.

FUNDAMENTAL 2: PRE-CALL PLANNING AND POST-CALL ANALYSIS

When my reps would pull up in front of the doctor's office, they would either reach for the car's door handle or for their computer. I was happy when I saw them reach for the computer. That told me that they planned their calls. They evaluated sales data and notes before making a call. If they reached for the door handle, I knew they were not planning their calls. This lack of planning is usually consistent with lack of sales. Since you may only get a minute to sell to your doctor, you want to maximize that time by planning an effective call.

Before you walk into and office, you need to ask yourself, *what do I want to accomplish during the call?* This is the essence of a pre-call plan. It's no different from when you go on an interview. You would ask yourself, *what is the goal of this interview?* It would either be to get another interview or to get the job. This planning will increase your chance of getting that second interview or the job because you will be certain to ask for it. Think about it, how many times have you left an interview without asking for the job and not getting it? Same with a sales call: the better you plan and ask yourself what you want to accomplish, the better chance you will ask the doctor to write prescriptions for your product.

Pre-call Planning entails reviewing and developing the following to create a plan to sell yourself as well as your drug to a particular doctor for a specific patient type.

Review

- 2-Week Schedule
- Sales Data
- Post-call notes from previous calls

Develop

- A goal for the call
- A clear concise message
- Productive Questions
- Close: Ask for the business

First look at your 2-Week Schedule. It provides a snapshot of that doctor, showing you the specialty and rank for both products. Those are two important things to know before making the call. You won't use the same plan to sell to a cardiologist as you would with an infectious disease specialist, regardless of the product you are selling.

Knowing the rank tells you which product to sell first, if you sell more than one product. For example, Dr. Smith is ranked number 1 for Product A and 9 for Product B. That means you will sell Product A first and then Product B.

Even if you were selling only one product, you would still want to identify your most important doctors.

If your company does not provide sales data in your computer, but gives it to you as hard copy, then input market share numbers in your 2-Week Schedule so you won't have to look for your hard copies. Make room on your schedule by inserting extra columns. This way, you will have everything on one sheet of paper.

Second, use your laptop to review sales data and notes you may have taken from your previous call. Reviewing this information before making the call will help develop a plan that is specifically targeted to that doctor. If you know a doctor is writing 40% of your drug, then your presentation may differ from the one you would deliver to a doctor who is only writing 3% of your drug.

Be sure to review your notes you had taken during previous calls (some companies no longer allow call notes for liability reasons). You may have noted the doctor said something like, "I usually follow evidence-based medicine when choosing a drug."

It's always great to feed the doctor's own words back to him by saying, "Doctor, last time I was here, you said that you practice evidence-based medicine. I just wanted to show you that Bioflex is the only drug in its class with a landmark study showing a significant decrease in cardiac death."

Third, now that you know the doctor's rank, specialty and sales numbers, and have reviewed call notes from previous discussions, you need to figure out what you will say and show. You can use your sales aid, a study, or both. In the example above, if your sales aid shows that Bioflex is the only drug in its class with a study showing a reduction in cardiovascular death, then use that. If you know the doctor will give you the time, then use the study itself.

During this part of the pre-call plan, you should practice your presentation in the car with the actual words you plan to use. Practice with your sales aids until you are comfortable with both.

Your pre-call plan can be as simple as developing and practicing your first line, a question, and the right close. Predetermine how the doctor may answer your question and know where to go on your sales aid to help answer the question or an objection.

Get Your First Line Out

Sometimes reps have difficulty getting the call started. They stumble over their words and forget what to say. I either see the doctor get impatient or express sympathy. That's why it is important to determine your opening line during your pre-call plan. It can be as simple as, "doctor, last time I was here…" Once you get your first line out, the rest of the call usually goes well.

Determine the right close. Be sure to develop a plan to focus on a specific patient type and to ask for the business for a specific patient type. I always coach my reps to verbalize the close in the car. When they do this it increases the chance that they do it during the call.

You could also plan one or two questions to ask your

doctor to help engage them in a discussion. Just be sure the questions are productive and intelligent.

Having a plan is better than going in blind and winging it. Many salespeople do not pre-call plan; only the successful ones do. Or, they sample drop—they see the doctor, get a quick signature, drop samples, and then the call is over. It's difficult driving business this way.

Or a rep may ask a doctor, "Hey, Dr. Williams, how's Bioflex doing?" The doctor may say something like, "Oh, great, I use it all the time."

Then the rep will say, "Hey thanks, I appreciate it." Then he goes back to the car and looks at his sales data and finds that Dr. Williams hasn't written a prescription for Bioflex in six months and wonders why.

Post-Call Analysis includes:

- What you learned

- What you said and showed

- What the doctor said

- The result of what you and the doctor said

- What you are going to do next time

If your company allows post call notes, then *immediately* after the call, either type a summary in your computer or write notes of your discussion with the doctor and what you plan to do next time. Post-call analysis sets up your pre-call plan for the next call. The doctor may have asked you to get back to him with information or may have said something worth mentioning next time. Doctors will remember what they told you if you remind them. It will help them remember how to use your drug. You will be surprised at how much more information they will provide you when you feed their own words back to them. When the doctor provides valuable information about how he treats his patients, you should be taking notes and then typing them into your computer. Your post-call note could read as follows:

I delivered a message using the visual aid and closed by asking Dr. Barnes if he would use Bioflex for his next diabetic patient who had normal blood pressure. At first, Dr. Barnes did not commit. So I asked him what percent of his diabetic patients was not hypertensive. He told me about 20% of them. I told him that Bioflex could further reduce the risk of cardiovascular death in his diabetic patients that have normal blood pressure, according to the HAAP Trial. Dr. Barnes said if I showed him data supporting that, he would consider putting his diabetic patients on Bioflex who did not have hypertension. In the meantime, I closed him to use Bioflex for his diabetic patients with high blood pressure and he agreed. Next time show the HAAP trial and get him to agree that diabetic patients with normal blood pressure should be on Bioflex.

As a rep, I always enjoyed opening the next call feeding the doctors' own words back to them. In the book *Warfighting, the US Marines Corps Book of Strategy,* F. Lee Bailey, a former marine and trial attorney (most famous for defending OJ Simpson) recalls a case he was prosecuting. He attended and listened to public speeches of a high-level executive from the company he was trying to prosecute. When he met with the executive to discuss a settlement, Bailey fed the executive's own words back to him and had him admitting to very damaging testimony. In the book, Bailey stresses the importance of always being prepared. When feeding a doctor's own words back to him, it can sound something like this:

> *"Doctor, last time I was here, you said that 20% of your diabetic patients did not have hypertension and that you would consider putting them on Bioflex if you saw data supporting that Bioflex can further reduce the risk of cardiovascular death in those types of patients. I brought you the HAAP Trial...."*

FUNDAMENTAL NUMBER 3:
EFFECTIVE USE OF LITERATURE

(*Visual Aids, Selling aids*, and *Detail pieces are often used* interchangeably). Experts say that people remember only ten percent of what they hear and more of what they see. Use those visual aids because doctors remember more of what you show them about your products rather than just what you tell them. Sometimes a doctor just needs to see the dose of the drug to write a prescription for it. If they forget the dose, they won't write for the drug. Sometimes they remember the drug by the colors and graphics on your visual aids. New reps shy away from using the sales aids. They think they can make a bigger impact by only talking. I was guilty of this myself. Sales aids provide a road map of your product and highlight the main selling points of your drug.

I learned the power of using selling aids when I started selling a pink-and-white anti-inflammatory drug; let's call it Opex. The selling aid complimented the colors of the capsule, which one of my doctors noticed during a sales call. She said, "Oh, you're the Opex rep?"

I said, "Yes, Doctor, I have been *telling* you that for the last three months!"

She told me that a patient wanted a prescription for

the little pink-and-white capsule because it was the only one that worked for her arthritis. The doctor hadn't written the prescription for Opex because she didn't know which drug the patient was talking about until she saw my detail piece. If I had showed her the Opex detail piece during those first three months, she probably would have written more prescriptions for it.

During another Opex call, a doctor said, "I notice he's working with ice."

I said, "What?"

He pointed to the detail piece that I was holding at my side rather than up towards the doctor's face where it should have been. It showed a black man about fifty years old working with huge blocks of ice. The doctor told me that a patient had just complained of hand pain from working with ice at the Newark waterfront.

After those two incidents, I always used my visual aids. They help paint a picture of different patient types that help doctors to visualize how to use your drugs. When a patient tells a doctor that they want the "purple pill," the doctor knows which drug the patient wants.

When using your (new, clean, unmarked) visual aids, be sure to use a pen to point to the different features and graphics. Some reps use their fingers to point. Jewelry or bad hygiene could distract the doctor from the message. Some reps don't point things out at all. When you're making a point, be sure to lead the doctor's eyes on a particular location on your selling aid.

Also, be sure to use visual aids that are not marked up, worn, dirty, or ripped! I'm still amazed at what some reps show their doctors. Just as you would not show a soiled or torn résumé, you would not show a doctor a detail piece in the same condition. This is a direct reflection on you—unprofessional and dirty! Order new detail aids regularly.

Don't read directly from your visual aids. You want the message to sound natural and uncanned. Use the visual aid as a guide, not a crutch, incorporating it in the discussion. If a doctor asks a question, and the answer is in your visual, then go to that part of the visual aid to help answer the question. If you only have time to deliver a few quick points, then point to the most important features of the drug and the dose. Tell the doctor a story, using your pen and visual aid to orchestrate.

If your visual aid has three or more pages, and you find it appropriate to use all the pages (especially with a new product), be sure to transition to each page. Don't stop talking while turning the page. It interrupts the flow of your presentation and will appear rehearsed. As you start flipping to the next page, make eye contact and start making your next point that will appear on the next page. This shows the doctor that you know your stuff. You should point to the dose as you are closing the call. This shows the doctor how to write a prescription for your drug.

Position your visual aid where the doctor can see it. If you are standing next to the doctor, then stand as close to him as possible and position the visual aid right under his nose. If you are sitting across from him on the opposite side of his desk, then position it on his desk and start pointing. Do not lose control of the visual aid by handing it to the doctor. Once you do that, you have lost control of the call. The doctor does not know where to look. If the doctor takes it from you, then gently take it back and show him what you want to show him.

Using Studies

If you are presenting a study, be sure to identify the journal, the date it was published, the lead investigator, and the title. Some reps just go right to the part in the study about their drug without properly introducing the source of the information. This is important to the doctor because the journal may be a respected source of medical literature. If the article was published fifteen years ago, the doctor may not consider that as up-to-date information.

Introducing the study could be this simple:

"The HAAP Trial, which stands for the Heart Artery After Prevention, was published in the New England Journal of Medicine in January of 2004. The lead investigator was Dr. John Heart."

Once you've introduced the journal article, summarize it in less than sixty seconds, eventually getting to the results. For example:

"The HAAP Trial evaluated the effects of Bioflex and Vitamin C on high-risk patients with heart disease. There were over five thousand diabetic patients with high blood pressure who were 55 years or older. The conclusion showed that Bioflex reduced the risk of heart attack by 30%, stroke by 40%, and death by 20%."

Another helpful tip is to use the author's name during your summary. For example, "Dr. Heart randomized only high risk patients and found that..."

After reviewing the study, don't forget to close!

"Dr. Baldwin, will you prescribe Bioflex for your diabetic patients with normal blood pressure?"

In summary:

- Introduce the Journal and Title of the article
- The publication date
- The author(s)
- Patient types and number of patients in the trial
- Results of the trial
- Close, ask for the business

FUNDAMENTAL 4: FOLLOWING THE PLAN OF ACTION

Most pharmaceutical companies hold two large sales meetings each year usually called Plan of Action (POA) meetings. During these meetings, salespeople practice delivering new selling messages for each product. Since most doctors do not have much time to see reps, it's important for reps to be able to deliver a quick, clear, concise message using a visual aid.

It's important that doctors hear a consistent message. We expect a doctor in New York to hear the same message as a doctor in California. Fundamental 4 means sticking with the key selling points discussed during these meetings, with few deviations. The consistency of the right message will increase the likelihood that a doctor will remember the key selling points. As a result, he will write more prescriptions for your drug for specific patient types.

Deviations from the core, selling message, such as unnecessary introductions, words, or questions, usually abort the presentation before it even starts. When a doctor allows a salesperson time, then they should just start selling by delivering the first line of the presentation that will hopefully develop into a discussion.

Instead, some reps might say something like this: "Doctor, I'm here to talk you about Bioflex."

Immediately, the doctor would say, "I'm using your drug," and walk away.

Some reps might say, "Doctor, I know you've heard this before, but…"

Or they might start with a ridiculous question: "How's Bioflex doing?"

The doctor would answer, "Great! Now where do I sign?"

Some reps do a great job delivering presentations, but can't sell a thing. They forget the reason they were hired. The presentation, as well as pointing out the features and benefits of the product, is designed to engage the doctor in a discussion about how he or she can use the product to treat his or her patients. A rep needs to ask questions and overcome objections to further involve the doctor in a discussion before finally asking for the business.

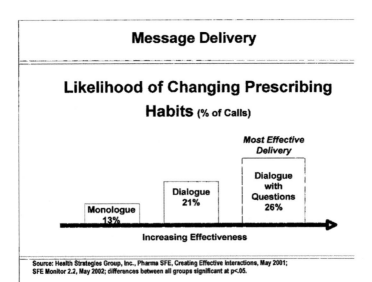

Message Delivery

Likelihood of Changing Prescribing Habits (% of Calls)

Most Effective Delivery

Dialogue with Questions
26%

Dialogue
21%

Monologue
13%

Increasing Effectiveness

Source: Health Strategies Group, Inc., Pharma SFE, Creating Effective Interactions, May 2001; SFE Monitor 2.2, May 2002; differences between all groups significant at p<.05.

The "Message Delivery" Chart shows that when a sales representative does most of the talking (monologue), only 13% of calls may result in a change of a doctor's prescribing habits. When a rep engages a doctor in dialogue, the likelihood increases to 21%. The most effective message delivery and change of prescribing habits occur when a rep engages a doctor with productive questions with dialogue.

Ask Questions

Ask questions to uncover concerns a doctor may have about using your drug and to engage him in discussion. It's better to ask questions during the middle or the end of the presentation. Asking a question as an opener may turn your doctor off. Asking questions during the middle gets the doctor thinking and may help engage him and paint a patient profile. You could ask questions right from the start if the doctor doesn't allow much time to sell and you want to try to engage him immediately or if you have a good relationship with the doctor.

We are looking for objections or reasons the doctor would not use the product. For example: "Based on this evidence, when choosing to write for an ACE-inhibitor, is there any reason or any types of patients where you would not use Bioflex?" The doctor may have a legitimate reason for not using your drug. However, their objections are usually smokescreens—excuses rather than real reasons they are not using the drug.

For example, after you've asked a doctor why he wouldn't use your drug, he may tell you that his patients develop a cough. This is a smoke screen reason not to use Bioflex, because cough is a side effect of all ACE-inhibitors. You can then say, "I meant when choosing an ACE-inhibitor, is there any reason you wouldn't use Bioflex?"

Either way, here is another way to overcome this

objection: "Doctor, as you know, cough is consistent with all ACE-inhibitors. What percent of your patients cough when prescribed an ACE-inhibitor?"

"Oh, only about ten percent."

"OK Doctor, let's talk about the ninety percent of your patients who don't cough.....When you do decide to prescribe an ACE-inhibitor for those patients who don't cough, will you then use Bioflex?"

Another common objection is that managed care health plans don't cover your drug. Here is a way to overcome this objection:

"Doctor, Bioflex has similar coverage as the rest of the drugs in its class. It's covered on eighty percent of all managed care plans. So will you prescribe Bioflex for those patients who are covered on your managed care plans?"

You should practice overcoming objections during pre-call planning in the car. Your responses should be automatic. Most reps stand there and have nothing to say. Don't be a deer in the headlights! (*See more on asking questions in Chapter Seven*).

FUNDAMENTAL 5: CLOSE THE SALE

Your close should be determined by your pre-call plan. Be sure to plan a specific close for a specific patient type.

After delivering a message, asking good questions, and overcoming objections, I see reps pause, hesitate, add unnecessary words and phrases, or just thank the doctor for his or her time— everything but ask for the business!

You can't rely on your great relationship or your ability to deliver presentations to get business. The success of the call is ultimately determined by your ability to convince a doctor to write prescriptions for your drug. The presentations and questions are precursors to the success of the call. If you don't ask doctors to write prescriptions for your drug, they won't. The other salespeople who do will get your business.

Some doctors will tell you that they will write for your drug as long as you visit often and leave plenty of samples. Don't believe them—they tell all reps that. Maybe they will increase from writing 1% of your drug to 3%.

When you have finally developed the courage to close and ask doctors for their business, shut your mouth and listen. Doctors will either commit or object. Either way, listen up. I see too many reps talk after they close because there is an uncomfortable silence. Make the doctor uncomfortable because you deserve an answer. If you don't allow him to reply, you are letting him off the hook. If that happens, you will not get a commitment.

Some doctors pause to think before answering. Give them time to gather their thoughts. Don't jump in! After a few uncomfortable seconds of silence, most reps can't take it and break the silence by saying something stupid like, "Well, Doctor, I'll leave you some samples." Some reps break the silence by holding out their hand for a handshake. Give the doctor a chance to answer!

Sometimes doctors start to reply and reps cut them off. This is when I imagine myself covering a rep's mouth. I'm in disbelief when they finally get the doctor to answer and then they interrupt them. Shut up and listen!

Chapter Four

The Mackay 66

KNOW YOUR CUSTOMER

The Mackay 66 is a selling tool from Harvey Mackay's book, *Swim with the Sharks Without Being Eaten Alive*—a must-read for any salesperson. It helps you gather personal and professional information about your customers to help you sell. Information won't help you sell unless you use it. I used this tool as a rep and currently to better understand my managers and salespeople.

One of my districts conducted over 250 birthday celebrations for their doctors and staff members and as a result, those reps owned their offices! Sometimes they baked cookies, brought doughnuts and coffee, or even a birthday card, whatever it took to own the office. That meant that these reps almost always gained access to their doctors where other reps did not. The result usually meant better relationships and more prescriptions.

I continue to use this tool as a sales director because my managers and salespeople are my customers and I want them to do the right things. The more I know about my salespeople, the better I will be able to sell them on my ideas. Mackay's book includes 66 things to learn about your customers. Below is a shortened version of what you should know about your doctors and their office staffs.

Melfa 24 for Doctors

Doctor's Name:
Specialty:
Date of Birth:
Office Address:
E-mail Address:
Home Address:
Office Hours:
Best Days & Times to See:
Office Staff Names & Birthdays:
Marital Status:
Spouse's Name & Occupation:
Spouse's Birthday:
Children: Names, Ages, Birthdays:
Hobbies:
Hometown:
High School:
College, Medical School, Residency:
Fellowship:
Sports or other School activities:
Someone He or She Admires Most:
Favorite Movie:
Favorite Book:
Favorite Food:
Musical Preferences:

Doctor's Name: If you work in a territory with diverse cultures, your doctors' names may be difficult to pronounce. Go the extra mile and learn how to properly pronounce a doctor's name and always address a doctor by his or her name preceded by "Doctor." Show them the respect they deserve!

Birthdays: You would think that other sales reps would know the doctors' birthdays and use this powerful tool to gain access in offices—most don't! The best reps are those who gain access and develop the best relationships with their doctors and staff. A birthday celebration can simply entail bringing a birthday card for a doctor or one of his staff.

During one of my birthday celebrations as a rep, I brought a birthday card and a couple of boxes of Dunkin Donuts (plastered with my product stickers) to a doctor's office. The doctor had not arrived yet, so I told the nurses and office staff that it was the doctor's birthday and that I would be back later.

Later that day, I ran into one of my colleagues. He asked me, "What did you do to Dr. A?"

I thought I had done something wrong and said, "Nothing much, I brought him a card and doughnuts and I'm going over there right now."

My colleague responded, "Dr. A was in a great mood because the entire clinic was wishing him a happy birthday. He had tears in his eyes because of what you did!"

What I did? I spent ten bucks on doughnuts and a card. I thought all reps were doing this. My colleague also told me that Dr. A was going to write prescriptions for all my products that day. Now, that's what I really wanted to hear.

When I finally returned, the nurses told me how happy I had made the doctor. I was a celebrity in that office. When I finally saw Dr. A, he reached out to me as if he was going to hug me, but then stopped himself and settled on a handshake. We discussed my products in detail—making sure he would know exactly the types of patients for whom he could prescribe my products. For two years, I celebrated the birthdays of everyone in that office, and for those two years, I owned that office!

Hobbies: In his book, Mackay tells a story about how top businessmen from the U.S., including himself, traveled to Cuba to try to do business for U.S. companies. He noticed that Castro was using a translator when speaking to other U.S. businessmen. Mackay did his homework and learned that Castro loved bowling. When Mackay reached out to shake Castro's hand, he rubbed his shoulder and told Castro he had hurt his arm bowling. Castro, without the help of his translator, started speaking English to Mackay. They hit it off so well that Castro invited Mackay to his house to bowl in his private bowling alley.

Although most pharmaceutical reps can no longer take doctors golfing or bowling, they can share hobby experiences instead of the activity itself. For example, rather than taking a doctor golfing, you can discuss an article on golf. You can be creative without spending money or breaking company rules.

During one of my calls on a doctor, I noticed a variety of elephants in his office. No, I wasn't hallucinating. Some elephants were wood-carved and others were ceramic and plastic. This doctor, although a nice guy, was not writing many prescriptions for my product. Every time I would start a product presentation, he would cut me off and tell me he was using my product.

During this call, rather than start with a product presentation, I asked him about the elephants. "Hey, Doctor, who was it who fought wars on elephants?"

His face lit up and I knew I had him. "It was Hannibal," he said.

After discussing Hannibal for about ten minutes, we

then briefly discussed my products. That night, I researched Hannibal and printed out a few pages about his war strategies. The next day, I left the pages with his secretary (who was also his wife). I told her I would like to return the next day to discuss Hannibal and elephants with the doctor. When I walked into his office the next day, the Hannibal printout was the only thing on his desk. No patient charts, no drug information, just my Hannibal printouts. We discussed Hannibal and elephants for about a half hour and I still had time to sell my products. As a result, he wrote an elephant-sized share of my product—a 50% market share!

You can learn a lot about a person by simply observing their surroundings. Train your eyes to absorb everything in an office. Look for pictures, paintings, props and degrees—anything that could spark a conversation and you can use to sell.

After I'd made several visits to one of the top-prescribing doctors in my territory (let's call her Dr. D), Dr. D still didn't even know my name. One day I noticed a picture of her and her husband ballroom dancing. The receptionist told me that Dr. D loved ballroom dancing. I had friends from high school who were well known in the dance community. I decided to mention my high school friends to Dr. D at her annual Christmas party. After competing with twenty other reps for a seat next to Dr. D, I asked her if she knew my friends. Not only did she know them, they were also dance instructors for her and her husband! She even reacquainted me with my high school friends. I began to attend dance contests and other social events with Dr. D. As a result, I gained access to her on every call. She would even sometimes stop her discussion with other reps and run over to me. This didn't make the other reps happy, but, hey, it's war out there.

Dr. McCampbell was another busy and hard-to-see doctor in my territory. But like Mackay, I did my homework.

I learned that Dr. McCampbell had written a novel and was hoping to publish it. I had just self-published my first book, *Bodybuilding: A Realistic Approach.* When I finally met with him, I said, "I heard you wrote a book." He looked up and smiled. We discussed his novel and eventually my products. I was one of the few reps who knew he had written a book and who had read it! Of course, I gave him a signed copy of my book and some tips on self-publishing. Speaking of writing, Dr. McCampbell wrote many prescriptions for my drugs. And better yet, we became great friends.

SEEING NO-SEE DOCTORS

As far as I'm concerned, there is no such thing as a no-see doctor. The more Mackay 66 information you gather and the more you use it, more doctors become accessible. Gather information by simply asking questions.

After many failed attempts to see Dr. No-See, I learned from his office staff that his four-year-old son was about to turn five and that the doctor was a car fanatic. I brought two Matchbox cars (which cost one dollar each) in a little bag with some candy from a local grocery store. I gave the bag to the office staff with a short note asking the doctor if I could meet with him.

Bingo! According to the office staff, I was the first rep to see the doctor in a year. I felt like Bud Fox finally getting to see Gordon Gekko in the movie *Wall Street.* After a brief conversation about his son, I asked him to use my product. As a result, not only did he write prescriptions for my product, I was the only rep who saw him regularly.

After a while, the staff wouldn't let me see him anymore until Halloween. I brought cookies and snacks for the office staff and Halloween candy for the doctor's son. I put the candy (which cost me two dollars) in a plastic pumpkin. I asked the office staff if I could see the doctor because I wanted to personally hand him the pumpkin for his son. One of the office staff told me that four other reps had tried to see him that day and that he had turned them all down.

"But did they bring candy and a pumpkin?" I asked. After a little more schmoozing, they got the doctor to see me again.

"Hey Doc, I got your son some cool stuff."

He told me my timing was great because his son was sick and wasn't going to get to trick or treat with the other kids. He also hadn't had time to get his son anything for Halloween. He called me a hero.

I told him, "Hey, Doc, you're making me a hero with all the prescriptions you're writing."

You could also try to see doctors in hospitals if you can't see them in their offices. You would be surprised of the time "no-see" doctors give you in the hospitals. (See *Chapter Five* for more on no-see doctors).

THE DANGERS OF NOT KNOWING YOUR CUSTOMERS

Knowing birthdays and hobbies and using that information can help build relationships with your doctors and office staff. Not knowing the most obvious things about your doctors can jeopardize sales.

In the book *What They Don't Teach You at Harvard Business School,* the author, Mark McCormack recalls a meeting with the famous John DeLorean. At the time, DeLorean was head of Pontiac and one of the most powerful men in the automobile industry. McCormack was selling a marketing campaign that would associate Pontiac with the U.S. Ski Team.

DeLorean sat at one end of the table and McCormack at the other. A group of young sports entrepreneurs sat scattered around the rest of the table. Between were all these nervous-looking ad-agency executives. As McCormack recalls, "I had the deal in my back pocket—I was feeling invincible." The idea was to use Pontiac's logo—an Indian head, which had been the company's symbol for many years—to tie in with the U.S. Ski Team.

"I totally winged it," said McCormack. As McCormack spoke of Indian heads and logos, he noticed many nervous eyes darting back and forth from him to DeLorean. McCormack sensed that no one was impressed with his idea and finally decided to shut up.

After a long moment of silence, DeLorean smiled and said, "Mark, you really researched the hell out of us. Pontiac's just spent a little over $3 million getting rid of the Indian head symbol and developing a new logo."

Invincibility just went out the window. The deal went through anyway, but McCormack admits that, after that, he was never so unprepared for a customer.

I experienced something just as embarrassing with one of my doctors. Soon after training, I was ready to discuss with my doctors what I had learned about my blood pressure drug. I thought I had perfected my presentation. I had studied all the literature my company had provided and practiced my presentation in front of a mirror. It was time for the real thing.

I was delivering a beautiful presentation to a doctor. After about one minute of flawless presenting—hitting on every major feature, benefit and advantage—I moved in for the close. "Doctor, will you use this drug on your next newly diagnosed hypertensive patient?" I was so proud. *If only my manager could see me now. I was closing!*

As in the DeLorean and McCormack meeting, there was a moment of silence. The words left the doctor's mouth as if she were speaking in slow motion. "I'm a pediatrician," she said.

I always wondered just how red my face glowed that day. How many four-year-old children do you know with high blood pressure? At the very least, I should have known her specialty. All I had to do was look at her business card, or even the word "pediatrician" plastered all over her walls and degrees. Like McCormack, I vowed never to be so unprepared for my doctors again.

I require all my salespeople to know and include the doctors' specialties on their 2-week and daily schedules and to review that information as part of their Precall-Plan (*See Targeting and Planning and Pre-call Planning in Chapter Three*). Knowing something as simple as the doctor's specialty could make a big difference between a good call and a bad one. I told you about a bad one. Here's a good one:

During a pre-call planning session with my one of my salespeople, we learned the doctor was not only a gastroenterologist, but also an oncologist (a stomach doctor and cancer doctor respectively). Our heartburn drug was not known to interfere with any other drugs. That's important if a doctor has a patient who is taking multiple medications— especially a cancer patient.

During the pre-call plan, my rep and I were strategizing how to drive home the no-known-drug-to-drug interaction feature of our product. I asked my rep what she knew about her doctor. From studying her previous call notes, it appeared the doctor thought that all the heartburn drugs worked the same. I kept asking her questions until she figured out that cancer patients are on many drugs. Since our heartburn drug was the only one with no known drug-to-drug interactions and since the doctor thought they worked the same anyway, why would he choose another drug like ours that might interact with other drugs? That was the selling message and the close.

My salesperson executed the plan and it went something

like this: "During our last call, you said that you thought most of the heartburn drugs work the same. No doubt all the drugs in this class are very effective in relieving heartburn. However, I sometimes forget that you are an oncologist, and I would imagine that many of your cancer patients are on multiple medications. HeartburnX differs from the others in its class because it has no known drug-to-drug interactions. So when you choose to write for a heartburn drug for your cancer patients who are on multiple medications, will you choose HeatburnX?"

The doctor looked up at me and said, "Now, that is a good job of selling and that is why I have been prescribing more of your drug." I beamed with pride.

I would grill my reps with questions about their doctors before we made a call. Most of the time they had the answers and sometimes they didn't—this I find unacceptable. If you don't know the types of patients your doctors treat, then how on earth will you sell to them?

During the last several years, pharmaceutical companies have established guidelines and restrictions about what salespeople can and cannot do with their doctors. Most companies have done away with golfing, sporting events, and other forms of entertainment. Most events must include an educational component. Be sure to check with your manager if you are uncertain of your company's guidelines. It's not worth losing the job that you worked so hard to get!

Chapter Five

Your First Office Call

BE PROFESSIONAL; BE PREPARED

Before you make your first call, be sure to be prepared. I'm still amazed at the lack of preparation I see, not only with new reps, but with veteran reps as well. When I ride with reps, I expect them to be fully prepared.

Be prepared, not only when you are on your own, but especially when you ride with your manager. Make a checklist before you leave your house. It should include the items listed below. And if you are riding with your manager, be sure to clean the car! (See more on field rides in Chapter Six).

- Calendar or Planner

- Daily Schedule

- Samples

- Sample Receipt Forms

- Visual Aids

- Reprints

- Business Cards
- Name tag
- Gas up Car
- Change for Meters
- E-Z Pass (toll card if you live on the East Coast)

Some reps think they can do this job without a calendar. You will be scheduling lunches, breakfasts, appointments, dinner programs, birthday celebrations, and various types of meetings. I have seen reps double-book lunches and miss appointments and sales meetings. If you have poor planning and organizational skills and managed to get hired, then work on improving these skills by reading books or attending a course. Chronic disorganization will get you fired.

Get yourself a good planner with a To-Do list and keep it with you always. I highly recommend using a Palm Pilot or Palm phones. They are much more portable than a bulky planner, and you can back up all your information on a PC or laptop.

Develop a daily schedule from your 2-week schedule (*See Targeting and Planning in Chapter Three*). Do not just wing your day. You should know in order which doctors you plan to see during the day.

Be sure your car is fully stocked with samples, sample receipt forms for the doctors to sign, visual aids, studies, change for parking meters, and anything else you can think of to be fully prepared.

Many reps go to their storage units in the morning and load up the car with samples and selling materials. If you are riding with your manager, be sure to organize yourself the day before! You won't have time to do it in the morning. You do not want to be late when meeting your manager, and never take your manager to your storage unit or a gas station!

Before you enter that office, be sure that you are wearing your name tag and have business cards. The office staff will usually ask you for your business card that will usually include your product names on the back of the card. If you want the doctor and staff to remember your name, then wear your name tag.

YOUR FIRST OFFICE CALL

Your goal on your first office call is to introduce yourself to the office staff and doctor, and to leave samples. If you are a new sales rep, be sure to let the receptionist know. She may allow you to see the doctor just because you are new. The receptionist will usually help you by providing information, such as office hours, sampling policy, birthday list, and just about anything else you need to know about the office and doctor. Be sure to ask for that birthday list!

When meeting the doctor, introduce yourself and your products. Since you are new, he or she will know not to ask you technical questions about your drugs. Milk the "new rep" thing as long as possible.

However, when given the opportunity to sell, start selling! At least know a few points about your drug, such as the indications, dose and side effects. Be prepared with your sales aid to show the doctor something, even it's just the dose of your drug. You can even use a sample box as a visual aid. Never pass up an opportunity to sell!

I learned the hard way during one of my first calls as a new rep. The doctor asked me which product I was selling. I provided him with the brand name of my drug. He was not familiar with the brand name and asked me for the generic name. I didn't know! "I'm new," I said.

He looked at my pen and answered his own question.

All I had had to do was look at my pen! It had the brand and generic name and the dose of my drug. Ignorance in this case was not a good excuse.

Once you have completed your call, be sure to have your sample receipt form or computer ready for the doctor to sign. Do not waste the doctor's time. And do not ask doctors where to leave the samples. They did not go to medical school and complete a residency and fellowship, to be asked where the samples should go. Check with the office staff about where to leave the samples. Once the call is complete, gather your things and leave.

THE GATEKEEPER

Your manager hired you because of your personality and your ability to connect with people. Here is when you get to use your personality. When you first approach the person in the window, smile, say hello, introduce yourself, and get her name. Be sure to address the gatekeeper by her name every time. This may sound trivial, but I know some reps that have been calling on offices for almost a year and still don't know the gatekeepers' names. We call this person the gatekeeper because she is usually the one who decides whether you see the doctor.

Tell the gatekeeper it's your first visit, give her your business card, and ask her if you can introduce yourself to the doctor. Most doctors see reps anytime during their office hours, some see you only during specific days and times, a very few require an appointment, and some claim not to see reps at all. If the receptionist tells you that the doctor doesn't see reps on that day, that's when you milk the "new rep" thing. Respectfully ask, since you are a new rep, if you could introduce yourself and leave samples. You don't want to be too aggressive the first time, but it doesn't hurt to ask. It's hard to say no to a new rep, especially one who is respectful and smiles.

GATHER MACKAY 66 INFORMATION

During the first few calls, start gathering as much information about the office as possible (*See the Mackay 66 in Chapter Four for more details*). Start with the basics: office hours, best times to visit, names of office staff, and a list of everyone's birthday. Some people may think this is too much for a first visit, but I think you can make an impact immediately, especially if someone's birthday falls during that week or month. It would be great to follow up with a birthday card.

Before you start asking questions about the doctor, first show interest in the staff by asking questions about them. You want to show them that they are just as important to you as the doctor. Remember, the gatekeeper decides whether you will see the doctor or not. If you want to know the doctor's birthday, first ask the receptionist hers. Then you could follow up and say, "Oh, by the way, when is the doctor's birthday?"

Also, try not to walk into an office empty-handed. Use the pens, pads, calendars, and other promotional items your company provides. If you run out of giveaways, then bring coffee, doughnuts, bagels, candy, or pastries. Go the extra mile!

INTRODUCING YOURSELF TO THE DOCTOR

When you meet the doctor, first address the doctor by name and title. Don't just say, "Hello, Doctor, I'm Frank with Pharma," or "How ya doin'?" The doctor is not your buddy. Instead: "Hi, Dr. Jones, I'm Frank with Pharma."

Be sure to smile and hold out your hand and shake firmly. If it is an elderly doctor with a frail hand, then be sure not to squeeze too hard. I have seen doctors pull their hands back as if they had just caught them in a vise grip. Then again, you don't want to give them the dead-fish handshake either. This all may sound trivial to you, but I have seen reps not smile or address a doctor with little respect. Always present yourself professionally.

Most doctors will allow you to briefly introduce your products. During the first call, you may not want to go into a full presentation. You will have other opportunities during future calls. To sell or not to sell depends on how the doctor sees you. For example, if he invites you to sit in his office and appears to be relaxed, then it may be an appropriate time to deliver a brief presentation about your products and engage the doctor in a discussion. If you are standing in the hallway, then you may just want to quickly mention the name of your product, the dose, and maybe one quick feature or benefit. It could sound something like this:

"I promote Drug X for hypertension. The starting dose is 5mg. I will also be leaving you samples of Drug Y for heartburn. Next time I come back, hopefully we can discuss them in more detail. It was a pleasure meeting you and I look forward to seeing you again."

Eventually (within the next two or three calls), you want to deliver full presentations and ask for the business (*See Chapter Three, The Five Fundamentals.*)

Most doctors like meeting new reps. Some doctors may ask about your family, schooling, and other personal information. This is a good opportunity to get to know the doctor on a personal level and work on your Mackay 66.

SAMPLES

By law, you need a doctor's signature (or in some cases, another licensed healthcare professional that can prescribe pharmaceuticals such as a nurse practitioner) to leave samples of prescription drugs. A common question is how many samples you should leave. One may argue against leaving too many samples because doctors sometimes give patients too many samples without a prescription. I'm a proponent of leaving plenty of samples after every call regardless of whether the doctors need them or not. I find that doctors will write more prescriptions when you leave plenty of samples. I notice that competitors with the highest market shares provide plenty of samples after every call.

Samples are excellent visuals for the doctor. If a patient needs a prescription and the doctor sees your samples in his closet, on his desk or on the counter, there's a good chance that he will use your product. Samples are great reminders for doctors to prescribe your drug.

You need to get your products in front of doctors' faces every time. You can even use your samples as a visual aid while you are selling. Show them the dose on the box. Take the sample out of the box. Sell the size of the sample, show them the color, and finally hand it to them and ask them to prescribe it!

THE SAMPLE CLOSET

Be sure to position your samples in the closet where the doctor can see and easily reach them. Often, there may already be a place for your samples, but you can always shift things around slightly. Office workers do not like it when reps shift samples, but if you show them respect and ask them if you could change your spot, they will usually allow it. Competing reps sometimes hide your samples or position their samples in front of yours. It's important to maintain your spot in the sample closet during every visit. It drives me crazy when my reps see competing drugs in front of our samples and do nothing about it. "I guess they just want the business more than you do," I would say.

Get a signature from the doctor regardless of whether or not you leave samples. The signature buys a few more seconds to sell or to make one more point, especially if you sell more than one drug. The next thing you know, the doctor may ask you a question about that last selling point which can result in a discussion.

Take care of your samples while you are waiting for the doctor. Some reps do that after they meet with the doctor. You may at times wait thirty minutes to see a doctor. Use that time by taking care of the samples first. When you complete the call with the doctor, you are out the door walking to your car rather than filling the sample closet. When you get to the trunk of your car, refill your sample bag and prepare for your next call—this saves time. Remember, the more calls you make, the more successful you will be. Always *think* ahead to your next call.

The No-See Doctor

You scored 100s on all your exams in training; you studied your products and know them better than your manager; your bag is loaded with samples; your sample sheet or computer is ready for the doctor's signature; and you're prepared to deliver that presentation you perfected in training. You walk into a doctor's office and the receptionist tells you that the doctor doesn't see reps.

As I mentioned in Chapter Four, as far as I'm concerned, there is no such thing as a no-see doctor. It may take some persistence, either by using the Mackay 66, or seeing the doctor elsewhere, such as at a hospital. Try going back the next day with bagels and coffee. Be sure to bring cream cheese and butter, and don't forget knives, plates, and maybe some orange juice. This may not initially work, but keep trying. One of my reps tried several times before he learned (using the Mackay 66) that the doctor couldn't start the day without an egg and cheese sandwich from his favorite deli. One morning, the rep brought him the sandwich and the doctor finally agreed to see him. The doctor spent about ten minutes with my rep discussing products and then told him that he didn't trust reps because of a bad incident he'd experienced with another rep. My rep assured him that he valued integrity and would present only accurate information.

Some doctors may not see reps in their office, but that doesn't mean they won't see reps. Ask the receptionist which hospitals the doctor sees patients. If the doctor is a cardiologist, then look for him in the cardiac catheterization lab. This is where cardiologists perform heart procedures. From my experience, they always stop in the lounge for a cup of coffee. Most hospitals allow reps to camp out in the doctor's lounge. You can do the same with a gastroenterologist. They also perform procedures, such as endoscopies and colonoscopies, and stop for coffee between patients. Internal medicine doctors also have a lounge. You just have to track them down. If I couldn't find them in the hospital, I used to page them; they always answered the hospital page.

You can also invite doctors to educational programs. Many need continuing medical education credits (CME) to maintain their board-certified status. If the doctor won't see you, then leave him a note with the program information. You would be surprised how many doctors will get back to you and attend.

Lastly, ask the gatekeeper if the doctor has an e-mail address. Many doctors prefer to communicate through e-mail. Once again, doctors have often replied to my e-mails. E-mails sometimes allow you the opportunity to ask doctors yourself when they will be in the hospital, when the best time would be to see them in their offices, and invite them to educational programs.

Chapter Six

Field Rides with Your Manager and Sales Director

These were my expectations as a manager when I rode with my reps.

- Be on Time

- Be Prepared

- Think about It the Day Before

- Two-Week Routing and Daily Schedule

- Computer Charged (bring cords, battery).

- Stock car with Samples & Literature day before we ride.

- Don't ever take me to your Storage Unit or Gas Station!

- Goal of day: Not to make a lot of calls. Coach and develop you. Be receptive

- Full Precall Planning and Post Analysis

- Execute the 5 Fundamentals on every call
- Feed me

Be on Time: When I left my district manager position for a sales director role with another company, my reps bought me a going away present. It was a beautiful clock with an engraving that read, "On-Time is Late!" How much more can I say about being on time for interviews, meetings, and especially field rides with your manager. As I mentioned early in this book, plan to arrive 15 minutes early. Showing up late for a field ride with your manager gets the day off to a bad start.

On average, you will only ride with your manager twice a month. For those two days you want to impress your manager as much as possible. So suck it up, get out of bed an hour early, and plan to have a great day.

Think about It the Day Before: Don't just wing your day with your manager and hope you have a good day. Prepare a checklist of what you will need to prepare for the day and what behaviors your manager will expect to see. Most good managers will provide you with a list of their expectations. Review them the day before the field ride.

Be Prepared: The first thing I want to see when I ride with a rep is a printed daily schedule with at least 10 doctors on it. The daily list of doctors should be in the order that you plan to call on them. I also want to see a Master 2-Week Schedule (*See Fundamental One in Chapter Three*).

You should also be prepared with your most recent sales numbers and previous field coaching report (better known as FCR) with completed follow-up plans. Your manager may ask you to follow up on some action items during and after a field visit. Be sure to take notes, complete the action items by the dates showed on the FCRs.

It never fails: We are trying to review sales data on the computer and the battery dies. Be sure to charge your computer the night before, bring your car charger, and an extra battery. This should be part of your checklist.

You should have the common sense to never take your manager to your storage unit or a gas station. Stock your car with samples and literature and gas up your car the day before your field ride.

Goal of Day: Not to make a lot of calls. Coach and Develop You. Be Receptive

Most successful salespeople are Type-A. They are eager to make as many calls as possible and don't like anything getting in their way, including their managers. Try to understand, your manager is there for a reason. The goal of the day is not to make a lot of calls, but for your manager to coach you and make you even better. That does not only mean your manager providing you with feedback on what you can be doing better, but a good manager will catch you doing things right. So slow down, and let your manager do his job. This includes conducting thorough Pre-call Planning and Post Analysis (see Fundamental 2 in Chapter Three).

Execute the 5 Fundamentals on Every Call: If you are wondering which behaviors your manager is looking for then read Chapter Three. They want to see that you are calling on the right doctors the right amount of times that you are planning your calls, selling with your visual aids, and asking for the business. These are the behaviors that your manager observes, critiques, and documents on the field coaching report.

Feed Your Manager. Most managers like to eat. So be sure to plan time for lunch. This also provides an opportunity to discuss how the day is going.

The Sales Director Field Ride: When riding with the sales director or anyone from the home office, be sure to accommodate that person. Don't look at it as an inconvenience but rather an opportunity to shine.

Normally, sales directors don't ride with poor performers unless they are getting ready to fire them. Sales directors usually ride with top performers. They do not want to waste their time with bottom feeders.

Given that, offer to pick the sales director up at the hotel at 8:00 am. Don't ask them to meet you somewhere and do not use the excuse that you don't have doctors to see that early. That's what I call a career ending statement. Find somewhere to bring them. Hospitals are open for business all-day every day with plenty of doctors to visit.

Your sales director may want to sit and talk first. That should take about 30 to 60 minutes. This is also an opportunity to review your sales performance and your future goals with the Company.

Be sure to be as prepared for your sales director as for your manager. Remember, your sales director is evaluating your manager more so than you. This is an opportunity to make your manager look good. Your actions are a direct reflection of your manager.

And lastly, don't end the day before 5:00 pm. That's even worse than suggesting starting the day after 9:00 am.

Chapter Seven

Sell, Don't Tell!

ASK QUESTIONS

Most doctors do not like questions from reps, unless they are productive questions—questions that make them think about their patients, questions that engage them in intelligent medical discussions. The better you know your product, the better questions you will be able to ask and the more credibility you will gain from your doctors.

Ask productive questions that are open-ended, so the answer won't be yes or no. For example, let's say you sell a cardiovascular drug that is proven to reduce heart attacks and strokes. Rather than just firing off facts about your product, you can ask a question such as,

"Doctor, when you put your patient on a cholesterol drug and it works, by what percent would you lower your patient's risk of a cardiovascular event?"

Most doctors (especially cardiologists) know that putting their patients on a cholesterol drug could lower their risk of a cardiovascular event by up to forty percent.

I notice that when reps ask doctors good questions, they

look up. This immediately tells me the doctor is engaged and searching for the answer. Most times, they will provide you with an answer, if you let them.

In this example, if you have engaged the doctor in discussion, you can then tell him that adding your drug to the cholesterol drug can further lower the risk of a cardiovascular event in his patients by thirty percent. This strategy works much better than just *telling* the doctor about your product.

Some doctors think that most drugs in the same class all work the same and would provide the same benefits to their patients. This ideology is called a "class effect." For example, all cholesterol drugs (called statins) lower cholesterol. But only your drug has a study showing that it reduces cardiovascular events in patients with normal cholesterol. You would want to know if your doctor thinks the reduction in cardiovascular events was specific to your drug or if he thinks that any drug in the same class would do the same. If that is the case, then just ask. The answer in this case will be either "Yes," "No," or "I don't know."

In this case, a one-word answer would be fine because it will allow you to convince the doctor to think otherwise. For example:

"Doctor, do you think the reduction of cardiovascular events in this trial using Drug A was a class effect?"

"Yes."

"Well, Doctor, let's say it was a class effect, but at what dose would the other drugs in the class provide the same results that Drug A showed in the trial?"

The doctor may think twice before using another drug other than yours in the same class because you made him aware of this information. Even though other drugs may work the same as yours, he really doesn't know which dose of the other drugs to use. This is called practicing "evidence-based medicine." He would just be guessing with other drugs. Many doctors, especially cardiologists, will use the drug with the evidence, regardless of whether they think it is a class effect or not.

Incorporate your questions somewhere in the middle of your presentation. This will allow the doctor to think about your product and its benefits first, unless it's one of those doctors who won't let you get past your first line. Then it would be appropriate to engage him immediately with a question. After asking one or two productive questions and engaging the doctor, close the deal!

"Doctor, when you choose to prescribe a statin, will you choose Drug A?" Then shut your mouth and wait for an answer. Many reps blow the call by not allowing the doctor to answer. (*See Fundamental 5, Closing, in Chapter Three.*)

DOCTORS LOVE TO TEACH

Ask questions in such a way that the doctor is teaching *you* something, rather than you trying to teach the doctor about your product. For example, during a call with a nephrologist (a kidney specialist), one of my salespeople was getting nowhere with what we call a "Yes-man"—a doctor who just says yes to anything you say without listening. When my salesperson started his presentation, the doctor immediately "yessed" him to death and then followed with, "Yes, I'm using your product."

After the call, we thought about our customer. We knew that nephrologists treat diabetic patients with kidney problems. We also knew that ACE inhibitors protect the kidneys, but we really didn't know how. As we developed our next call plan, I told my salesperson that *next time*, he should ask the doctor how ACE inhibitors protect the kidneys. I was thinking this question could engage the doctor in a discussion and we could learn something as well.

During the next call, the doctor was shuffling papers, reviewing patient charts—paying us no attention, as if we weren't even there. My salesperson then asked: "Doctor, how exactly do ACE inhibitors protect the kidneys?"

For the first time in six months, we saw a pair of green eyes behind the doctor's glasses rather than the start of male-pattern baldness. He stared at us as if to say, "Finally, a good question from a salesperson." He then ripped a sheet of paper from one of the patient charts, flipped it over and scribbled a kidney. Like a mad professor, he gesticulated at his drawing: arms flailed, eyebrows raised, and his green eyes came alive! Instead of just saying, "Yes," he sang medical terminology: words such as nephrons, glumerulus, efferent and afferent blood flow dripped off his tongue like the protein he drew in the urine. With his pen, he orchestrated the process of microalbuminuria leading to kidney failure. We engaged him!

We then executed our next carefully planned question: "Do all ACE inhibitors protect the kidneys in the same way?"

He said he wasn't sure. Then we got into a discussion about tissue-specific ACEs versus nontissue ACEs and asked him if it was possible that tissue ACE inhibitors protected the kidneys better than nontissue ACEs. He agreed that it was possible (one step closer to commitment).

Then we went for the close: "Doctor, when you prescribe an ACE inhibitor for your next diabetic patient, will you choose Anex?"

He looked up, then looked down at his drawing, and then back at us again (uncomfortable silence: shut up!) and then he answered, "Yes, I will."

LISTENING & CLARIFYING

Misunderstandings between a salesperson and a doctor occur too often, most of the time it's because the salesperson does not listen. Even when the salesperson is trying to listen actively (by shutting his mouth), he sometimes hears something completely different from what the doctor actually said.

Sometimes the doctor misinterprets what the rep is trying to say. Even when the doctor tries to confirm what the rep said and interprets it incorrectly, the salesperson agrees to the misinterpretation, because, once again, he was not listening. Reps are usually more interested in what they want to say, rather than listening to what the doctor has to say.

For Example:

Salespeople are trained to include the dose with the name of a drug when mentioning the drug. For example, if a drug called Bioflex is used in a 10mg dose, salespeople would call it "Bioflex 10mg," rather than just Bioflex. This is an effective way to get doctors to remember the dose of a drug.

Sales rep: "Doctor, Bioflex 10mg is the only ACE inhibitor proven to reduce the risk of cardiovascular death in diabetic patients. Given this evidence, will you prescribe Bioflex 10mg for your next diabetic patient?"

Doctor: "I don't want to start my patients on 10mg."

Sales rep: "But Doctor, in the trial they used 10mg, so you should use 10mg for your patients."

Doctor: "There's no reason for me to start at such a high dose. Higher doses usually mean more side effects."

The doctor didn't realize the salesperson had mentioned Bioflex 10mg only because he was trained to include the studied dose used in a trial. And since the salesperson did not understand and listen to the doctor's objection, he could not overcome it. He could have said, "Doctor, I'm not saying that you should start your patients on 10mg. You can start them at a lower dose and eventually increase to 10mg. I'm asking if you will use Bioflex instead of the other ACE inhibitors."

In another example, let's say you're selling a heartburn drug for patients who complain of nighttime heartburn. You could ask the doctor a productive question like:

"What percent of your patients actually complain of nighttime heartburn?"

Answer: "Well, very few of them experience breakthrough symptoms at night."

The doctor just provided a valuable piece of information. When he says that very few of his patients have "breakthrough" symptoms, he is actually saying that he already has his patients on a heartburn drug and, it is working through the night. If the salesperson listened to the doctor's response, he would know how to confirm and respond properly.

Salesperson: "Doctor, what you are telling me is that your patients are already being treated with another drug and are not experiencing heartburn symptoms at night, is that correct?"

Doctor: "Yes."

Salesperson: "What I meant to ask is how many of your new patients who are not on other drugs are complaining of heartburn symptoms at night."

When I hear my reps say, "Doctor I just want to make sure I understood what you said…." Or "Doctor, what I meant to say was…" then I know they are listening and clarifying.

The most effective heartburn drugs are called proton pump inhibitors (PPIs). The experts say that PPIs should be dosed in the morning before breakfast. Here's another example:

Salesperson: "So, Doctor, will you use Heartburn X for your patients who complain of nighttime heartburn?"

Doctor: "Does that mean I should dose it at night since they have symptoms at night?"

Salesperson: "Yes."

This is a good question from a doctor and an incomplete answer from the salesperson, because the salesperson didn't understand the question and didn't even try asking for clarification. This is a combination of bad listening skills and poor product knowledge. Most salespeople who sell PPIs know that these drugs should be dosed in the morning before breakfast. A doctor could dose it at night if he wanted; there would be no harm in doing so. But in this case, the salesperson is trying to convince the doctor that his product, when taken in the morning, lasts all-night, unlike some of the other products. And the doctor is trying to find out from the salesperson whether a patient who suffers from heartburn at night should be dosed with that drug at night.

A better answer would have been: "Doctor, all PPIs should be dosed in the morning before breakfast, regardless of when your patients complain of heartburn. Our studies show that Heartburn X works for the entire twenty-four hours when taken in the morning, so your patients may not need to take it at night. That's what makes Heartburn X so effective. So why don't you try dosing Heartburn X in the morning, and if your patients still complain at night, then you can consider dosing it at night. Will you give Heartburn X a try for your next patient who complains of heartburn at night?"

FEATURES, BENEFITS, AND ADVANTAGES

A feature of a drug is determined by its pharmacological makeup. For example, the pharmacology of a drug will allow for once-daily dosing (QD dosing). This is determined by the half-life of a drug, which means the amount of time until half of the drug is eliminated from blood stream. Area Under the Curve (AUC) is the amount of drug in the blood after administration of the drug. Other features can include its mechanism of action, or the way the drug works. For example, antidepressants can work in many ways. They can be serotonin reuptake inhibitors (SSRI) or serotonin norepinephrine reuptake inhibitors (SNRI) or they can inhibit dopamine levels in the brain. Telling a doctor that your antidepressant is an SNRI (a feature) may not help you much during that presentation. Unless you tell him what the benefit of that dual mechanism of action can mean for his patient.

The benefits of a drug are a result of features and what they mean to the doctor and patient. For example, let's say you sell an antibiotic that is QD dosing. This offers a great advantage to both the patient and doctor, because the patient only has to remember to take it once a day rather than twice (BID) or three times (TID) per day. What that means for the patient is that they will feel better faster, and the doctor won't get calls from his patients who forgot to take their second or third dose and do not feel better after three days of therapy.

One of the first things I learned as a new rep in training was how to sell the features and benefits over the competing drugs by saying, "Doctor, *what that means is...*" A lot of reps just rattle off the features of the drug and don't tell the doctor what the results mean for him and his patients. For example, reps would say,

"Doctor, Drug X only has to be taken once a day; it has a longer half-life and AUC than any other drug of its class; and it is a small tablet."

A good salesperson converts features to benefits. For example:

"Doctor, Drug X has the longest half-life of all the drugs in its class, *which means* your patient only has to take it once per day, *unlike* all the other drugs in its class, which are dosed twice per day. That means your patient is less likely to forget to take one pill once per day rather than two pills during the day.

What this will mean for you is fewer phone calls from your patients complaining that they are not getting better because they forgot to take their second dose."

In the antidepressant example above, the benefit of a dual mechanism drug such as an SNRI can mean relief of more symptoms of depression. The neurotransmitter serotonin is theorized to relieve emotional symptoms of depression where norepinephrine is believed to relieve physical symptoms such as headaches and muscle aches. This can mean a patient will feel better faster. Not only will they not feel emotionally depressed, but they may no longer have headaches and muscle aches. This would not only be a benefit to patients, but an advantage of one antidepressant over another.

The advantages of these features and benefits answer the question, "what does your product have over the competition?" Use the word "unlike" to compare your product with others, because it replaces many unneeded words and makes your presentation more concise and brief. And believe me, doctors want you to be brief. For example:

"Doctor Drug X does not cross the blood brain barrier unlike the other drugs in its class. What that may mean for your patient is fewer central nervous system side effects."

In this example, I used a drug's safety feature to convert a benefit and advantage where in the examples above I used a drug's efficacy and dosing features.

After effectively selling features and benefits gain agreement from the doctor. Gaining agreement from a doctor sets up the close. For example:

"Doctor would you say that many of your patients forget to take their medications when dosed more than once a day?"

"Would you also agree that a smaller tablet will be easier for your elderly patients to swallow?"

"Ok, then will your prescribe Drug X for your elderly

patients who have difficulty remembering to take their meds and have difficulty swallowing a larger pill?"

Or, "Doctor would you say that at least one half of your depressed patients complain of overlapping emotional and physical symptoms of depression?"

"Will you then prescribe Drug Y for those patients?"

Selling the features and benefits of your product also allows you to focus on specific patient types rather than a general patient population. It helps you paint a picture for your doctors of exactly where to use your product. You can always expand to other patient types once you get them to start using your product.

BRIDGING WITH FEATURES AND BENEFITS

Bridging is a tool used to transition from one product to another when you are selling more than one product. There are several ways you can bridge:

- Compare one product feature or benefit to another.

- Compare symptoms or diseases.

- Compare patient types.

You could use a drug's half-life as a feature. Half-life means how long it takes for half of the drug to be eliminated from the blood. Another feature could be once daily dosing. The benefit would be convenience to the patient.

After completing your first product presentation and then closing and gaining a commitment, you can then bridge to your second product. For example:

"Doctor, Sinax's long half-life means excellent tissue penetration and efficacy for your patients with sinusitis. Conversely, Oprex's short half-life means no drug accumulation, so if your patient has a bad reaction, it will be eliminated faster than other products."

This is much more effective than saying: "My other product is Oprex." The doctor may cut you off and tell you that he is using your other product. But if you sneak the other product in by bridging, the doctor won't even know what hit him. Instead, he may appreciate your clever selling skills.

An example of bridging a cardiac drug to an antidepressant using patient types and disease states could go as follows:

"I mentioned that fifty percent of the patients in the HEART Trial who were on HEARTX were post MI. What percent of your patients who have had heart attacks are now depressed? Well, Depress X shows excellent results for your depressed patients that have suffered a heart attack..."

TAKE HOME POINTS

- Rather than just saying, "My other product is..." instead bridge to your next product.

- Be sure to close and gain a commitment on the first product before bridging to the next product.

- Finally, take the extra minute in your car to practice your presentations, bridges, and closes, so you don't mess it up in front of the doctor.

Chapter Eight

Hospital Selling

My success as a field rep getting my antibiotic used in community hospitals helped launch my promotion to a hospital rep.

One main goal as a hospital rep is getting your drugs available in the hospital pharmacy so doctors can use them. That means getting them on a list called a "formulary." If your drug is not on the hospital formulary, then the doctors can't use it freely. And that means little or no sales. Doctors are limited to what medicines they can use in hospitals. Since hospitals are very cost-conscious, they have what is called a Pharmacy and Therapeutics Committee (P&T) or a Formulary Committee that decides what products are added to or removed from the formulary.

Cost is a big factor when the committee decides whether a drug is added to the formulary. The P&T Committee usually includes the Director of Pharmacy and a group of doctors. A doctor usually serves as the head of the committee, but you have to get the support of the Director of Pharmacy before anyone else. You could get everyone else to vote for your drug, but the Director of Pharmacy could still shoot it down because of cost.

Selling products in both community hospitals and large

teaching institutions is challenging, especially if you have to get a drug on formulary. Sometimes, if drugs are not on the formulary, doctors can use them on what's called a non-formulary basis. Doctors would then need to make a written request for the drug for each patient, which is something they do not like to do.

DUCKS IN ORDER

To get your drug added to the formulary, you have to get all your ducks in order:

- You first have to develop a relationship with the pharmacy staff.

- Then you have to sell the pharmacy director a need for your product and a better price than the competing drugs already on the formulary.

- Develop relationships with the doctors who sit on the committee. If you are lucky, they may be doctors you already call on and have relationships with.

- A doctor has to make a written request for the drug, to get it added to the formulary.

- You need to fill out forms and get them to the pharmacy before the big meeting.

Once your ducks are in order, the committee meets and votes on whether your drug gets approved.

When you are assigned to a hospital, luck sometimes determines how much money you initially make. For example, my antibiotic was not on formulary at any of my community hospitals. That meant that my first bonus check did not include any money from that drug. However, since my bonus was based on a fifty-percent market share increase, all I had to do was get my drug on formulary at one hospital to make some money. And this is exactly what I did.

MY FIRST HOSPITAL SUCCESS

My first success in getting my antibiotic on formulary wasn't easy. I first visited the hospital pharmacy. When I poked my head in the pharmacy window, the Director of Pharmacy almost chewed it off. She told me never to come down without an appointment—my first rookie mistake.

Telling her which company I was from and the product I promoted didn't improve my situation either. At the time, we had just merged with another company, which meant there had been a shuffling of territories and salespeople. She complained about not having seen a rep from my company for months.

To make matters worse, she told me that she and the infectious diseases (ID) doctor (who was also head of the Formulary Committee) were trying to put my drug on formulary but had not been able to contact anyone from my company. She then warned me not to even try to see the infectious disease doctor, because we were *persona non grata*. In other words, I was out of luck.

When I reported to my manager, he told me to follow up with the ID specialist anyway. I made a 9:00 a.m. appointment a few days later. After waiting for three hours, I was considering just forgetting it and leaving. After the way I had been treated by the pharmacy director and given she had told me not to try to see the ID doctor, I was ready to walk out. But of course, I didn't. Patience paid off big time and he finally saw me.

He did not apologize for making me wait for over three hours. His expression clearly said, "You have nerve even trying to see me, and I planned to make you wait as long as possible."

I first told him the pharmacy director had chewed me out and had told me not to even try to visit his office. He finally smiled and I knew I had him.

He explained in more detail why pharmacy had chewed my head off, which also explained why he had made me wait for three hours. He told me that my antibiotic was better than other drugs available in the hospital. He had wanted to add it to the hospital formulary but had not been able to contact a salesperson from my company before I was hired. In short, he was pissed off.

I told him that I wanted to start fresh and get my product on formulary. He agreed to help and provided me with the following instructions:

- See the head of microbiology to test my product against other antibiotics currently on formulary (this is called an antibiogram).

- Set up another appointment with pharmacy and make friends with them. (Without pharmacy's support, he assured me, my drug would not get on formulary.)

- Provide him with regular updates on my progress (follow up).

For eight grueling months, I followed up. Eventually, the entire pharmacy department welcomed me. I no longer needed appointments. Occasionally, I would bring pizza, bagels, coffee, and some pens and pads, and everyone was happy. The head of microbiology helped with the testing and my drug showed to be superior on the antibiogram, just as the doctor had said. I provided the doctor with updates, and in the interim, he used my product on a nonformulary basis. Eventually, my product was added to the formulary and shortly after that, I got it on formulary at three other hospitals!

My advice would be to focus on one hospital first to learn the process, because you will make mistakes. If you are new to hospital selling and try working on three hospital formularies at once, then you will likely make the same mistakes with all of them and lose all three hospitals.

Here is a checklist to cover before you or a doctor submits what is called a formulary request form.

THE FORMULARY APPROVAL PROCESS

- Meet with the Director of Pharmacy.

- Meet with a Pharm D.

- Find the formulary committee members.

- Find out the date of the next Formulary Committee Meeting.

- Get a Formulary Request Form from pharmacy.

- Get a doctor to fill out the form in his own writing.

- Submit the Formulary Request Form to pharmacy at least two weeks before the date of the meeting.

Meet with the Director of Pharmacy: You should always meet with the Director of Pharmacy first before doing anything else. Getting pharmacy's support is important, not only because the director is usually on the committee, but because they can always shoot down your drug because of cost. If you try to bypass pharmacy support, they could easily find a reason to shoot down your formulary request form.

Remember to take your time during this process. Don't rush this step. If your first meeting with the director does not go that well, don't let that discourage you. Pharmacists can be tough in the beginning. You need to win them over. Set up educational programs for the pharmacy staff, provide a good lunch during those programs, and learn all the names and develop a relationship with every pharmacy member.

When you meet with the Director of Pharmacy, be prepared. Know as much as possible about your drug and be prepared to discuss cost. If there is a contract based on performance, be sure you understand it. Here is chance either to gain credibility or lose it. Know what you are talking about! Be the businessperson and professional that you were hired to be. Ignorance is no excuse for failure!

Meet with a Pharm D.: A Pharm D. is a pharmacist with a doctoral degree in pharmacy. They are usually next in command after the Director of Pharmacy and influential in deciding which drugs get on formulary. If you are selling an antibiotic, you may find a Pharm D. who specializes in infectious diseases. Many times, they have the power to either help you or hurt you. So be sure to develop a relationship with that person.

There may be a different Pharm D. assigned to other drug classes, such as cardiology and gastroenterology. As I said before, learn everything you can about every pharmacy member and have your ducks in order before even asking for the formulary request form.

Find the Formulary Committee Members: You want to be careful during this search. Unless you have good relationships with pharmacy staff, you do not want to ask them questions about Formulary Committee members. The committee is supposed to be kept secret. The first people I would start asking are your doctors. If you have good relationships with your doctors, they could tell you just about anything you need to know. A doctor will always be the head of the committee and will probably be someone you know. If you are lucky, it may be one of your doctors.

Once you learn who the committee members are, try to meet with them to gain votes for your drug. Before you approach each doctor, try to learn something about each of them (*see the Mackay 66 in Chapter Four*). Some of them may not want reps to know that they sit on the committee. You don't want to jeopardize your chances by calling on people who don't want to be called on. Ask the doctors with whom you have relationships who you should see.

When you visit with the formulary members, sell them on features and benefits of your drug and why they should add it to the formulary. Depending upon the type of drug you are selling, you may get lucky again and find that some of these doctors already use your drug, either in another hospital on a nonformulary basis, or in their private practices.

I would visit with each doctor several times before making the formulary request. You want to be sure you have their support first. This may mean bypassing the first available formulary meeting and waiting an extra month.

<u>Find out the Date of the Next Committee Meeting</u>: In just about every hospital, the formulary meeting date is the same day and week of every month. For example, the committee may meet every third Wednesday of every month. Once again, ask only people whom you trust about the dates. The committee date is a closely kept secret, and usually held on the same day of each month. Sometimes the dates get postponed to the following month, so be sure to stay on top of it.

It's important to follow up with your advocates on the committee. Doctors habitually miss those meetings either because they forget or don't want to attend. You could have done all your homework up this point and blown your chances of success because you didn't remind your doctors to attend the meeting.

Get a Formulary Request Form from Pharmacy: There is usually one person in pharmacy responsible for scheduling the meetings and developing the agenda. This is the person who will tell you the deadline for submitting the form. Obviously, if you have made it this far, he or she will also provide you with the date. If you slack off and submit the form late, you will have just blown your chance! Once pharmacy makes the agenda without your drug on it, it will take an act of God to change it.

Get a doctor to fill out the form in his own writing: You want to get a doctor with influence in the hospital to make the request. This should be a doctor whom other doctors respect or even fear. Most pharmacy staff do not want a committee member to fill out the request because of conflict of interest. This may vary from hospital to hospital. In the past, I had the Director of Cardiology, who also sat on the committee, fill out a request for one of my cardiac drugs. Since he was influential, no one objected to his request and I got my drug on formulary.

Once you have selected your doctor, have him fill out the form in his own writing. You will also need to fill out the manufacturer's section of the form and it wouldn't look good if the handwriting was the same in both sections.

Submit all Forms Correctly and on Time: Be sure to submit the form on time, or else you will have to wait until the next formulary meeting. Although you may think you might only have to wait a month, formulary meetings can be postponed for months.

When you fill in the manufacturer's section of the form, don't skimp on any information; be as thorough as possible. Provide all information such as indications, cost, and studies. Be sure to include a package insert as well. Do not, under any circumstances, include any promotional materials, such as a detail piece or other Madison Avenue materials. Have either your manager or your medical affairs person review the form before submitting it. Do everything right the first time so you won't have to do it again.

Once you are sure you have everything filled out properly and have included all relevant information, put everything in individual folders. Don't skimp here either. A pharmacist in charge of the agenda once told me that committee members are impressed with a professional presentation from the manufacturer. Be sure to make enough copies for the entire Formulary Committee.

If you have done everything right and have all your ducks in order, then there is a good chance the Committee will approve your drug. And believe me, there is no better feeling I can think of during my career in pharmaceutical sales, apart from winning a President's Award.

Once you get your drug on formulary, start selling it. Don't let all that work go to waste. Don't get complacent, thinking your drug will get used just because it is on formulary, unless you were smart enough to negotiate an automatic formulary switch!

Formulary Switch: If you have negotiated and done your homework, sometimes, your drug will automatically get used even when another drug has been requested. The smartest reps with the best business sense will negotiate an "automatic switch." What beauty! What genius!

However, this does not mean you should slack off. Continue selling your drug as if that switch had never happened, because the enemy is at the gate. If you get complacent, the competition will come in and steal away your business.

RESIDENTS & Fellows

One big difference between community hospitals and teaching hospitals is that most teaching hospitals have residents and fellows and most community hospitals do not.

Residents are doctors that recently graduated from medical school and have to work in a hospital for three years until they can practice medicine on their own,

A Fellow is a resident doctor that completed a three-year residency program in a hospital and seeks to specialize in a particular medical field such as cardiology, gastroenterology, or infectious diseases.

In community hospitals, you sell mainly to the attending doctors (doctors who have graduated from their residency programs or fellowships and are now in private practice).

In most teaching hospitals, the residents and fellows do most of the prescribing because there are usually many of them and they are there all the time. The attending doctors are only there when treating their patients from their private practices.   In some teaching hospitals, the attendings still may make most of the prescribing decisions. It is up to you to learn your business and know whom to target. In large teaching institutions, there are many different types of residents. What you sell will determine which residents to target. For example, internal medicine and podiatry residents all treat patients with antibiotics.

Another big difference between selling in a teaching hospital and community hospital is there are more people to see in teaching hospitals than in community hospitals. You can spend an entire day in one teaching hospital calling on many departments with residents, fellows and attendings. There could be over a hundred internal medicine residents and another hundred surgical residents in one hospital.

Where Do You Sell?

- ICU
- CCU
- SICU
- Podiatry
- Resident Lounges
- GI Suite
- Cardiac Catheterization Lab
- Library
- Psychiatry Dept
- Oncology
- Hospital Clinics

Who Do You See?

- Residents
- Fellows
- Heads of Departments
- Attendings
- Education Administrators
- Director of Pharmacy

- Pharmacist & Pharm D's

The product or products you sell will determine where you will invest most of your time in a hospital. If you are selling an antibiotic, you can sell to doctors from just about every department in the hospital because they all treat various types of infections. I sold three IV drugs including an antibiotic, a cardiac drug, and one for acid suppression. Although I sold to everyone, I mainly targeted the residents and fellows. I started early in the morning, bringing the internal medicine residents doughnuts, bagels, and coffee. They have what is called a morning report, which usually started at 7:00 a.m. This is when a resident would present a case study to the rest of the group. Before the morning report started, I would briefly mingle and sell to each of the residents and then present to the entire group.

After morning report, I would target different departments and units, such as the ICU (intensive care unit) where the really sick patients were treated. I would then visit the CCU, the cardiac care unit, selling to cardiologists, and then to the surgical residents in the SICU (Surgical Intensive Care Unit). I also sold in the hospital library and cafeteria, both places where I found many of the residents.

I was successful selling my antibiotic to the podiatry residents. They always told me that no other reps visited them or sponsored any educational programs. And this was one of my largest teaching institutions in New Jersey. They were a neglected and untapped department in that hospital where I owned almost 100% market share. The other reps didn't understand that podiatry residents treat diabetic foot infections and start patients on IV antibiotics following foot surgery.

Don't forget to visit the various clinics in the hospital, regardless of what products you sell. The residents, fellows, and attendings treat various types of patients with various illnesses. When I sold in hospitals, I felt like a kid in a candy shop. I found residents everywhere! Residents all had their own lounges for each department where I often brought lunch and midday snacks. I also found them in the library and the cafeteria. I would sit and each lunch with them and sell my products.

You can visit the education department and heads of each department to set up educational programs such as grand rounds. Each department had their own grand rounds. For example, the cardiology department would bring in an expert speaker to lecture to the entire cardiology department in the hospital. The hospital reps would provide an educational grant to the hospital to help sponsor the speaker and lunch. The doctors who attended the grand rounds program would earn continuing medical educational credits. It's a win-win relationship for everyone.

Hospital selling was a terrific experience for me. It was a lot of fun and I excelled. Many hospital reps are promoted to district managers. Hospital reps have more experience with different types of doctors, hospital administrators, and organize various educational programs than office-based reps. If your goal is to be a manager, then I would urge you to first become a hospital rep.

Chapter Nine

How to Get Promoted

In Pharmaceutical Sales, there are many opportunities for promotion. Typically, you start as a territory sales rep. From there you can earn a promotion to either a specialty rep or hospital rep, depending on what products your company promotes. After four to six years of field and hospital selling, you can get promoted to district manager.

I have always thought that you are much more marketable as a hospital rep for a district manager position over a specialty position. You learn more business skills and meet with a larger variety of customers as a hospital rep over a specialty rep. (Be sure to read Chapter Eight to get a better idea of a hospital rep's responsibilities.) As a hospital rep, you learn how to get products on hospital formularies, meet with directors and staff of hospital pharmacies, interact with heads of different specialties, and with hospital executives. As a specialty rep, you do basically the same thing you did as territory rep.

You will need at least two years of successful sales performance that exceed your company's expectations for a promotion to any position. If your performance has been average or "At Expectations" I wouldn't even try. I have seen many reps with average performances repetitively interview for promotions, only to be rejected every time. Usually, the rep's district manager is too big of a wimp to tell them not to even bother, but I'll save that discussion for my next book.

Promotion Criteria

Performance: First, you will need consistent performance to be considered for a promotion. One quarter of good performance will not be enough. Your last two performance appraisals should read, "Exceeds Expectations" to lock in a promotion.

Express Interest: Some high-performing reps think that because they have the performance that others will seek them out for a promotion. When a promotion becomes available, many will express interest. If you just sit back thinking the hiring manager will come to you, then you are mistaken. First talk with your manager about your interest. You will need your manager's support and permission to interview for the job. Do not go over your manager's head.

Take on Extra Responsibility: Ask your district manager for extra responsibility. You would be doing your manager a big favor as well as marketing yourself for a promotion. You can ask to run a meeting or teleconference, sit in on interviews, run a journal club, roll up monthly sales reports. Ask and you shall get!

Field Trainer: Being a field trainer is an important step for promotion, especially for district manager. Sometimes this experience helps you to solidify your interest and decision on wanting to be a district manager. It did for me.

I became a field trainer during my third year as a hospital rep. I at first helped other new hospital reps in the district by spending a day with them in the field or them spending some time with me in the field. I would coach and provide advice on how to do the job based on my experience and observations in the field.

I knew I wanted to be a district manager when I went to the corporate office to help train new promoted hospital reps. I never had a group of people rely on me the way the new hospital reps relied on me during that week of training. They genuinely appreciated my help and wanted leadership.

That same week I ran into the vice president of sales who was my former regional sales director. He asked me what I wanted to do next. I told him based on my experience as a field trainer that I wanted to be a district manager. The rest was history.

This is another advantage of being a field trainer. You expose yourself to home office people. If you do a good job, several important home office people notice you and it opens other promotional opportunities.

Be a Good Role Model: You want to be known as a leader and a top performer in your district. Most top performers are hard workers. Also, follow this advice:

- Don't complain
- Always have a positive attitude
- Don't be a know-it-all
- Don't get complacent
- Never compromise your integrity
- Be a product expert
- Develop a Business Plan

Even if you are a top performer, but known as a complainer, it may cost you a promotion. Nothing I can't stand more is someone who complains. Leaders don't complain. You may get by with a promotion to specialty rep or hospital rep, but never to a district manager. If you complain, then that negativity will infect others. That's the last person a sales director wants on his team. Resist the urge to complain and always have a positive attitude.

Some top performers have done so well, that they think they can't learn anything from others. One of John Wooden's (famous UCLA basketball coach) favorite maxims is

"If I am through learning, I am through."

Always be receptive to learning something new and improving your sales performance regardless of how good it is. Never get complacent with your performance. I used to hear some reps say that they were going to take it easy during a quarter so the next quarter would be easy to reach goal. That's the dumbest thing I have ever heard any salesperson say. Always give it everything you got. That defines being a good role model and showing integrity.

Develop a Business Plan

In Chapter Two, I discuss that every rep should have a business plan that shows where you are, where you want to be, and how you are going to get there. If you are interviewing for a promotion, then develop a brief, 10-slide PowerPoint presentation. This should include:

The promoted position or territory's performance quarterly or yearly:

- Revenues

- Prescriptions (NRx or TRx)

- Market Share

- Rank

Where you plan to take it:

- Increase revenues from one million in 2007 to 1.5 million in 2008

- Improve quarterly prescriptions from 1000 to 1500

- Improve territory rank from 35 to 15 in 2008

- Win two formulary approvals at Hospital X and Y.

What you are going to do?

- Target only the highest potential doctors

- Be a product expert by studying my products every day

- Visit with the hospital pharmacy director the first week you hire me

- Ask Dr. Smith to fill out a formulary request form

- Schedule two educational dinner programs each month with the following doctors.

A brief business plan will differentiate you from the rest of the candidates fighting for that promotion. It will show your new boss, that you are smart, a good planner, and that you will drive business faster than anyone else.

Interview Questions

SALES ABILITY AND PERSUASIVENESS

- *Tell me about one of your biggest or most memorable sales.*

- *Tell me about a time when you persuaded someone to do something. What did you say?*

- *What are some of the best ideas you ever sold to a supervisor or a peer? What was your approach?*

Remember the STAR method in Chapter One—provide the situation, your actions and the results, and be as specific as possible.

- *What are some of the best ideas you tried, but failed to sell your supervisor? Why was the idea rejected?*

Be careful here! If you had a good idea, but your sales efforts failed, you better be able to provide a good reason why your efforts failed. A good answer could be that your

manager loved the idea, but he didn't have the budget to do
it. Failing to sell an idea is sometimes OK if you learned from
your mistake and were able to capitalize on it during a later
opportunity. For example, tell the interviewer that you didn't
close the deal because you didn't ask your supervisor to use
the idea. Then explain that you learned how to close and
were able to close him on other ideas.

- *What have you learned about sales in the past? What
  have been your key components to successful sales
  calls?* (See Chapter Three, The Five Fundamentals.)

- *Compare a sale you made to a sale you lost.*

Once again, be careful. It's OK that you lost a sale, as long
as you are able to show the interviewer that you learned from
a previous mistake.

- *Tell me about a time when you tried to persuade
  a group of people such as sorority members,
  classmates, or work colleagues to see your point of
  view.*

Pharmaceutical selling has changed since I was a rep.
I was the only one responsible for selling my products in
the territory. Most companies now use team selling. There
could be up to four people selling the same drug in your
territory to the same doctors. Someone must emerge as the
leader. That means setting up Pod meetings with an agenda,
getting everyone organized, and suggesting how to organize
calls. This is essential so Pod members are not going to the
same doctors on the same day. And you better be able to
sell your ideas or there will be chaos in that Pod. Have you
ever tried changing someone's schedule? Well try it with two
or three other people! Recently however, most big Pharma
companies are going back to the old selling model of one rep

for each doctor. But you still may need to sell your ideas and organize teams.

TENACITY

- *Can you tell me about an experience when you persisted toward a goal for a long period of time? What was the result?*

- *Tell me about a time when you successfully overcame objections to show how products or services met the needs of a customer.*

- *What is one of the biggest obstacles you've had to overcome to get where you are today? How did you overcome this obstacle?*

- *Tell me about a specific situation in which you stuck with a position or plan of action despite barriers or difficulties.*

Good examples are those where a candidate had been trying to land a big customer or make a big sale and had been repeatedly told *No,* but persisted until they finally landed the big customer or sale. If you don't have sales experience, you can use other examples such as making it on to a sports team, getting into a college class that was closed, finishing a project at school or at work that kept hitting roadblocks. You will need to search your memory. The point is to prepare yourself to answer these questions before the interview.

CONTINUOUS LEARNING

- *Tell me about a time you got information about a key competitor. How did you use that information?*

- *Have you taken any steps to improve your skill or performance? Give me an example of when you did this.*

- *What self-development actions have you recently taken?*

- *Have you ever had to learn new information about changing products, markets, or procedures? Tell me about one of those situations and how you learned the new information.*

- *What sales books have you read recently?*

See Appendix 2 for a list of books you can start reading now!

PLANNING AND ORGANIZATION

- *What did you do to prepare for today?*

I love asking this question. This is when you show everything you brought. Don't just tell me you went on the Internet. Show me your brag folder, the research you did on the products, interviews with doctors and pharmacists, and anything else you want to show me. If you went on a field visit with another company, then tell me about it.

- *Describe a situation that required you to perform several tasks at once. What did you do?*

- *We have had times when we just couldn't complete assignments on time. Tell me about a time when this has happened to you?*

- *When scheduling your time, how do you determine priority tasks? Can you provide an example?*

- *Has your schedule ever been upset by unforeseen circumstances? What did you do then?*

- *Do you have a system for organizing your work area? Tell me how that system helped you do your job?*

- *Tell me about a time when you had to adjust your priorities to make an important sales call.*

- *Can you describe a situation where someone needed files, records, or other material from you? How were your materials organized so you could find them?*

We sometimes use various questions to evaluate your organizational and planning skills. We need to know that you can develop a routing schedule with the right doctors at the right times, prioritize tasks and following up actions for your doctors and manager, schedule appointments and other meetings. You also need to show that you can organize your car and storage unit so you can easily find studies, samples, and other items important to doing your job. I had gotten so frustrated with one of my reps, I had to tape a list to his steering wheel, so he wouldn't forget to take anything into a doctor's office.

Show us how you use a planner and To Do List and how you prioritize tasks. If you are going to show your brag book, be sure to organize it. Practice running through it several times at home before the interview

If you have an experience where you couldn't complete a project on time, you can tell the interviewer that you made the effort by working extra hours and weekends. You can also say that you asked for an extension and eventually got the job done.

INTEGRITY

- *Tell me about a specific time where you were faced with an integrity issue? What did you do?*

This can be a tough question because you may have known about a past employee who was stealing from the company and had to decide to either do nothing or report it. On one hand, you wouldn't want to be known as a snitch, and on the other, by doing nothing, you allowed the person to continue stealing from your company. In this case, you could have decided to discuss the issue with the person that was stealing. Tell them that you have been aware of the situation and to stop because it was not worth losing their job.

- *On a scale of one through ten, how would you rate your integrity?*

You would be surprised of the number of people who provide answers lower than 10. When asked this question, answer 10 without any hesitation. If you have to think about it, then we have to think about the honesty of your answer. With all the Wall Street scandals such as Enron, WorldCom, Martha Stewart and others, most companies have a zero tolerance for unethical behaviors. Remember to always do the right thing. As the famous basketball coach, John Wooden used to say, *"Tell the truth. That way you don't have to remember a story."*

PROBLEM SOLVING

- *Tell me about a time where you had to solve a problem. What did you do to solve it?*

- *Tell me about a time when a customer presented you with a problem with a product and you needed to follow up.*

Nothing burns me more than when my reps do not follow up with their doctors. Doctors sometimes do not receive speaker materials, run out of samples, or request product information.

It's OK not to know how to solve the problem, but find out and solve it immediately. Many reps would let it go or would wait until I rode with them so I would solve it for them.

Previous Experience

- *What did you like most (or least) about your previous or current job?*

- *Tell me what your manager would say about you?*

- *Tell me about your relationship with your former manager.*

You need to consider that maybe pharmaceutical sales may not be for you. People tell me they hated the long hours of their previous job and want to work in pharmaceutical sales because they heard it had flexible hours. Trust me, if that is your reason for wanting to get into this industry, then search for another career. On the other hand, if you can honestly say you love the thrill of closing a sale, developing relationships, being recognized for your performance, and you can work well in a team setting, then you know that pharmaceutical sales is for you. Be sure to communicate these reasons to your potential boss.

In my many years of work experience, I have had few bad managers. The few bad managers had been in non-sales positions. In pharmaceutical sales, I was lucky to have excellent managers. If you worked in sales and were successful, then even the worst managers would have been happy with you as long as you performed. There were always salespeople that did not get along with my previous district mangers and those were the ones that usually had performance problems. My point is, don't bad-mouth your previous managers. If you worked for a bad manager, don't tell your potential manager about it.

Recommended Reading

Swim With the Sharks Without Being Eaten Alive, by Harvey Mackay

Success is a Choice, by Rick Pitino

What They don't Teach you at Harvard Business School, by Mark McCormack

What They Still Don't Teach You at Harvard Business School, by Mark McCormack

Samurai Selling, by Chuck Laughlin and Karen Sage with Marc Bockmon

Bodybuilding A Realistic Approach, by Frank A. Melfa

War Fighting: The U.S. Marine Corps Book of Strategy

How To Win Friends & Influence People, by Dale Carnegie

The Power of Positive Thinking, by Norman Vincent Peale

Straight From The Gut, by Jack Welch

It's Not About The Bike, by Lance Armstrong

The Exceptional Presenter, by Timothy Koegel

Beyond Success: The 15 Secrets to Effective Leadership and Life Based on Legendary Coach John Wooden's Pyramid of Success, by John R. Wooden and Brian D. Biro

Wooden, by John R. Wooden

Closers: Great American Writers on the Art of Selling, by Mike Tronnes

Developing the Leader Within You, John C. Maxell

The 7 Habits of Highly Successful People, by Stephen Covey

Who Moved My Cheese, by Spencer Johnson, MD

Taber's Cyclopedic Medical Dictionary, by F. A. Davis

Wall Street Journal

Pharmaceutical Representative, Advanstar Publication

Appendix 3

Check List for Successful Educational Dinner Programs

1. Get the speaker to commit to a date and time.
    - Get Tax ID #

    - Presentation Preference (round table, stand up)

    - PowerPoint Slides

    - List of possible attendees from doctors

2. Mark two dates in your calendar:
    - The date of the program

    - One week before to start planning and inviting

3. Change your Actual Schedule: Indicate doctors you need to follow up with that week. That includes the speaker, and doctors to invite.

4. Select a Restaurant
    - Reserve a Private Room if possible

    - Find out average cost per head

- Inquire about Preset Menu and wine list

- Screen Set up

- Let them know in advance that you need an itemized receipt.

5. Get the paper work in ASAP! Do not procrastinate.

6. Make invitations

7. Start Inviting: Do not wait until the day before to start inviting doctors. At the very least allow one week to get invitations out and follow up.

8. Contact your partners and POD members to help you invite residents and fellows.

9. Be sure to reserve an LCD projector

10. Buy and expense the following:
    - Extension cord

    - Pointer

    - Batteries for pointer

11. The day before the program, check with the restaurant to confirm your reservation and private room. Follow up with your speaker and make one last effort inviting your doctors.

Pharmaceutical Company Websites

3M Pharmaceuticals, mmm.com
Abbott Laboratories, abbott.com
Adams Respiratory Therapeutics, adamsrt.com
Alcon, alcon.com
Allergan Inc., allergan.com
Alliance Pharmaceutical Corp, allp.com
Alpharma Inc., alpharma.com
Altimed Pharmaceutical Company, altimed.com
American Pharmaceutical Partners appdrugs.com
Amersham. Health, amersham.com
Amgen Inc., amgen.com
Amylin Pharmaceuticals, amylin.com
Anesiva, anesiva.com
Apothecus Pharmaceuticals, apothecus.com
Ascend Therapeutics: ascendtherapeutics.com
Astellas Pharma US Inc., us.astellas.com
AstraZeneca Pharmaceutical Company, astrazeneca.com

Bayer Pharmaceutical Division, bayer.com
Berlex Laboratories, berlex.com
Biogen, Inc., biogen.com
BioMarin Pharmaceutical Company, biomarinpharm.com
Boehringer Ingelheim Pharmaceuticals, boehringeringelheim.com
Bristol-Myers Squibb, bms.com
Bausch & Lomb, bausch.com
Celgene Corp., celgene.com
Cephalon Inc., cephalon.com
CV Therapeutics, cvt.com
Daiichi-Sankyo Inc., dsus.com
Eli Lilly and Company, lilly.com
Ferring Pharmaceuticals: ferringusa.com
Frontier Pharmaceutical, frontierpharm.com
Fujisawa Healthcare, fujisawa.com
Genaissance Pharmaceuticals, genaissance.com
Genentech, gene.com
Genzyme Corporation, genzyme.com
Gilead Sciences, gilead.com
GlaxoSmithKline, gsk.com
ImClone Systems, inclone.com
Innovex, innovex.com
Inspire Pharmaceuticals, inspirepharm.com
Inventiv, inventiv.com
Isis Pharmaceuticals, isispharm.com
Johnson & Johnson, jnj.com
KV Pharmaceutical, kvpharma.com
La Jolla Pharmaceutical Company, ljpc.com
Ligand Pharmaceuticals, ligand.com
Medicines Company, themedicinescompany.com
Medicis Pharmaceutical Corporation, medicis.com
Merck & Company, merck.com
Millennium Pharmaceuticals, mlnm.com

Mission Pharmacal, missionpharmacal.com
Novartis, novartis.com
Noven Pharmaceuticals, noven.com
Novo Nordisk, novonordisk-us.com
Nycomed, nycomed.com
Ortho-McNeil Pharmaceutical Company, orthomcneil.com
Otsuka America Pharmaceuticals, otsuka.com
PDI Inc., pdi-inc.com
Pfizer, Inc., pfizer.com
Proctor & Gamble, pgpharma.com
Progenics Pharmaceuticals, progenics.com
Prometheus Laboratories, prometheuslabs.com
ProStrakan, prostrakan.com
Roche Pharmaceutical Company, roche.com
Salix Pharmaceuticals, salix.com
Sanofi-Aventis, sanofi-aventis.com
Salix Pharmaceuticals, salix.com
Savient Pharmaceuticals, savientpharma.com
Schering-Plough Corporation, scheringplough.com
Schwarz Pharma, schwarzusa.com
Shire Pharmaceuticals, shire.com
Sepracor, sepracor.com
Serono Inc., seronousa.com
Solvay Pharmaceuticals, solvaypharmaceuticals-us.com
Stiefel Laboratories, stiefel.com
TAP Pharmaceutical Products, tap.com
Teva Pharmaceutical Industries, tevapharm.com
Valeant Pharmaceuticals, valeant.com
Vertex Pharmaceuticals, vpharm.com
Watson Pharmaceuticals, watsonspharm.com
Wyeth Pharmaceuticals, wyeth.com

Glossary

Ace Inhibitor: A blood pressure lowering agent that works by inhibiting angiotensin I from converting to Angiotensin II which prevents vasoconstriction of the blood vessels. ACE's are also used to preserve kidney function in diabetic patients.

Angina: Chest pain caused by clogged arteries.

Angioplasty: A procedure performed by a cardiologist where he inserts a mesh stent in a clogged artery then balloons it, enabling blood flow through the artery.

Angiotensin Receptor Blocker: Sometimes called the new Ace Inhibitors—they lower blood pressure by blocking the angiotensin receptor rather than inhibiting the conversion of angiotensin. The two most popular ARBs are Cozaar® and Diovan®. ARBs decrease the incidence of cough.

ARBs: See Angiotensin Receptor Blocker

Atherosclerosis: A build-up of plaques in the arteries. A form of cardiovascular artery disease (CAD).

Attending: A doctor who treats patients in a hospital that has completed their residency or fellowship.

AUC (Area Under the Curve): The amount of drug in the blood throughout a drug dosing interval.

Beta Blocker: A blood pressure lowering agent that decreases heart rate. Lopressor® and Toprol® are well-known beta blockers.

BID Dosing: Twice a day dosing of a drug.

Blood Pressure: The force of blood flow on the walls of the arteries. The top number is called the systolic pressure and the bottom number is called diastolic pressure.

CABG (Coronary Artery Bypass Grafting): Heart surgery where a clogged artery is bypassed with a healthy one.

CAD (Coronary Artery Disease): Progressive narrowing of the arteries caused by plaques and inflammation. Atherosclerosis is a form of CAD.

Calcium Channel Blockers: Blood pressure lowering agents that block the calcium channel receptors in the heart. Norvasc® is the most popular calcium channel blocker on the market.

CCU (Cardiac Care Unit): A unit in the hospital where cardiac patients are held. Patients can include post heart surgery patients, heart attach victims, CHF, and other heart problem patients.

Cardiac Catheterization: A procedure performed by a cardiologist where a catheter is inserted in the leg and travels to the coronary arteries to view the arteries and the heart. This procedure is usually preceded by chest pain.

Cardiac Catheterization Lab: A location in the hospital where catheterizations are performed.

Cardiologist: A medical doctor that has completed a fellowship in cardiology.

CHD (Coronary Heart Disease): Heart disease defined by any of the following: high blood pressure, heart failure, angina, heart attack, left ventricular hypertrophy.

CHF (Congestive Heart Failure): A condition where the heart loses its force to pump blood, causing blood and fluids to pool in the lungs.

Colonoscopy: A procedure performed by a gastroenterologist where a tube is inserted in the rectum to view the large intestine.

Decile: Numbers used to categorize the volume of prescriptions doctors prescribe. A Decile 10 is the largest.

Diabetes: There are two forms of diabetes: Type I and Type II. Type I is juvenile onset where the body does not produce insulin. Type II is adult onset where the body produces insulin, but it doesn't work properly. The muscles are unable to use glucose for energy. As a result, sugar builds up in the blood causing many forms of organ damage.

Endocrinologist: Is a specialist in metabolic diseases such as hyper or hypothyroidism. Endocrinologists also treat a large number of diabetics.

Endoscopy: A procedure performed by a gastroenterologist where a tube with a tiny camera is inserted in the mouth to view the esophagus for damaged.

Fellow: A medical doctor who has completed a residency program in a hospital and seeks to specialize in a particular medical field such as cardiology, gastroenterology, or infectious diseases.

Formulary: A list of drugs a doctor can use in either a hospital or a health care plan.

Formulary Committee: A group of doctors and pharmacists that make decisions on drugs to add to a hospital formulary. This is also called a Pharmacy and Therapeutics Committee.

Gastroenterologist: A medical doctor who has completed a fellowship in Gastroenterology and specializes in diseases from the esophagus to the rectum. They also specialize in hepatitis.

Half Life: The amount of time it takes for half of the drug to leave the body.

Heart Failure: See Congestive Heart Failure.

Ischemia: A reduction of blood flow to vital organs

Ischemic Attack: When a reduction of blood flow results to a stroke or heart attack.

Intensive Care Unit (ICU): A unit in the hospital where very sick patients are monitored on a twenty-four hour basis. Patients include those with serious infections such as pneumonia and HIV.

LVH (Left Ventricular Hypertrophy): Enlargement of the left ventricle, usually caused by untreated hypertension. LVH if left untreated can lead to congestive heart failure.

Macroalbuminuria: A condition where protein (greater than 300mg) accumulates in the urine, caused by kidney damage from hypertension and diabetes.

Market Share: The number of prescriptions written by a physician for a product divided by the total number of prescriptions written for that drug class by that physician.

Microalbuminuria: Small amounts of albumin found in the urine—a marker for cardiovascular heart disease.

Myocardial Infarction: A heart attack—blockage of blood
   flow to the heart.

Nephrologist: A medical doctor who specializes in the
   kidneys.

Nephrons: Small filtering units of the kidneys.

Nephropathy: When the kidneys start to fail as a result of
   damaged nephrons. Kidneys can no longer filter wastes.

Oncologist: A medical doctor who specializes in cancer.

Pharmacy and Therapeutics Committee: A committee
   of doctors and pharmacists in a hospital that make
   decisions about drugs that get added and deleted from
   the formulary.

Proteinuria: See macroalbuminuria.

Proton Pump Inhibitors: A class of drugs that inhibit acid
   production by shutting off pumps in the stomach that
   produce acid.

PTCA (Percutaneous transluminal coronary angioplasty):
   See angioplasty.

QD Dosing: Once per day dosing of a drug.

Residents: Medical school graduates that work in hospitals
   for a minimum of three years.

Script: Another word for prescription.

Statins: Drugs that lower cholesterol such as Lipitor® and
   Zocor®.

Stroke: Also known as a brain attack—a blockage of blood
   flow to the brain.

Surgical Intensive Care Unit: A unit in the hospital where
   post surgical patients stay

TIA (Transient Ischemic Attack): A mini stroke.

TID Dosing: Three times a day dosing of a drug.

Index

Notes

Notes